Wild
in the
Hollow

Wild in the Hollow

On CHASING Desire
and Finding the
Broken Way HOME

AMBER C. HAINES

Revell

a division of Baker Publishing Group
Grand Rapids, Michigan

© 2015 by Amber C. Haines

Published by Revell
a division of Baker Publishing Group
P.O. Box 6287, Grand Rapids, MI 49516-6287
www.revellbooks.com

Printed in the United States of America

Library of Congress Cataloging-in-Publication Data
Haines, Amber C.
    Wild in the hollow : on chasing desire and finding the broken way home /
    Amber C. Haines
        pages cm
    Includes bibliographical references.
    ISBN 978-0-8007-2407-8 (pbk.)
    1. Haines, Amber C. 2. Christian biography—United States. I. Title.
    BR1725.H158A3 2015
    277.3′083092—dc23   2015010359
    [B]

Some names and details have been changed to protect privacy.

Published in association with literary agent Jenni L. Burke of D. C. Jacobson & Associates, an Author Management Company, www.dcjacobson.com.

In keeping with biblical principles of creation stewardship, Baker Publishing Group advocates the responsible use of our natural resources. As a member of the Green Press Initiative, our company uses recycled paper when possible. The text paper of this book is composed in part of post-consumer waste.

15 16 17 18 19 20 21   7 6 5 4 3 2 1

For my kin:
Seth and our boys
and every child who comes after.

Contents

CONTENTS

Introduction

THE HOMESICKNESS

If you were to meet me in person, the first thing you'd notice is the green from my mama's eyes and the prominent nose from Daddy's sprawling Scotch-Irish and Native American line. If we were to speak, I wouldn't be ashamed of my honeysuckle drawl, the sense of home that drips from my mouth.

If you were to see me as a child, you'd see me with my sister, our manes a tangled mess, wind-wild in saw-briar woods. We never knew then to relish our age. We only woke in our time like babies in a blanket unfolding. I had grandmothers in three directions, baby brothers, and good cousins. We had a canoe in the yard and the lake down the road. We caught crawdads and sang "Blue Moon of Kentucky" while Daddy played guitar. The sky turned navy, and the whip-poor-will called us in. We were Alabama girls in the dirt, Alabama girls lying down on the front steps. We knew the safety of a gentle mama. Dark came, and the woods crawled, always a snap from something hiding within them. Eyes glowed everywhere. We knew the settled way, the silence within, and we knew how to listen in the dark.

The sky looked like a sea of bats, and under their darts, we would close our eyes and let the cicadas and an Audubon's variety of frogs lift us into the hum and heartbeat of wild song. And then we would listen deeper. "What do you hear?" we would ask. An owl, rustling leaves, a truck door down the road, coyotes by the dozen: invisible things were everywhere, but we knew how to hear.

There had been a death in our house decades before us. A great-aunt had an aneurism. There was an attic, and I always wondered if she watched me from its window above. I knew that snakes lay in the dust. The crow's shadow always weaved through the limbs. We were never terribly afraid but stayed close enough to hear and to eat from the garden.

Once I dangled from our Appalachian Mountain on a tire swing, my hands choking the rope, body spinning fast round. The pines climbed to heaven and shivered, letting go the needles. I was in the safe, invisible arms, my Father's world. Then the terrible scream of a wildcat echoed into the hollow from right nearby, and I fell and hit the ground as the wind picked up in a furious howl, chasing me into the house, then blowing down the hill through a field of bitterweed. The wind took up the small places, the black knots in dead wood and the frilly powdered undersides of mushrooms. The maypops and pecan hulls, every one encased by the wind, their scents rode on it and pushed at Mama Lois's rippling pond while cattails danced. There's something out there. I knew it then, and I know it now—something bigger and other. The terrible and the beautiful are watching me.

The invisible has always been as real to me as the smell from behind the barn—the hogs and then the sweet mix from the pile of chestnuts that Peggy Israel's mama gave us. I always knew there was more than what my eyes could see. Maybe that's why it's easy for me to imagine Eden. I have my own version, the place where I clearly remember my early childhood experience as beautiful, wild, and protected.

I wonder if I know a little of what Adam and Eve may have felt, or at least I like to imagine it. Adam had a home with God, who was still on his breath. He couldn't have known how marvelous it was simply to unfold and speak in holy tongue. God taught original language there but let Adam choose what to call the animals. When he woke to Eve, I wonder if he thought her like a dove. She wasn't made from the ground like the rest but was made of his bone, strong. He loved her. He loved how he fit with her. They were whole there together at home, where a million metaphors began, all the ways to experience God.

They were naked by the river, listening, legs sprawled out the way kids sit wide open in front of their mamas, no shame. The sky was a sapphire and full of water. They were in the freshness of God's rest: easy sleep and fulfilling work.

When the angel came with the flaming sword in every direction, sending them away from the Tree of Life, what grief must have pressed in. This is where our inherited sense of homesickness began. The clothes they hadn't needed before were sewn by the hand of God, and then the babies came, and with them violence, rejection, and enough shame to send the world into needing a flood.

How they must have looked back and remembered. How they must have missed home. When Adam's plants bore no fruit, did he close his eyes and taste Eden's pomegranates?

I wonder if he was like I am. When the seasons change, anything shifts at all, it reminds me of home. I long for it. I can taste it. I've been known to wake up early in the morning, imagine the biscuits, and start packing my four sons in Arkansas to drive all the way to Alabama. I get sick with missing, but every time I go, it doesn't seem to have the same sweet feeling as the one I had as a child. Not many even know my name there now, and the sense of freedom I used to have isn't any easier there than it is here. It often doesn't stop me from trying though. I long for a place to fit, and sometimes I forget and become desperate for a sense of peace. I want to hear my daddy say my name. I want to listen to the creek run white over rocks with my sister. I want my children to feel the wind sweep through.

All the striving to regain such feelings of home, even as I create home now as a wife and mother, I know none of it will do to give me peace. Home here really is a mere metaphor, but it's one that anchors me. How wild and free we were when we were too small to care for ourselves in that hollow at the mountain base. The way I remember home is the same way the prodigal son remembered his when he found himself eating scraps. It's the place we know we can go, where we'll be received and fed. It's where we know we have a name.

I'm not so naïve to think that most people have lovely childhood memories of home like I do. I think we were the only people on the planet to have a ginormous swimming pool slide in our yard without the actual pool at the bottom. Even still, I wonder if you feel it too—the homesickness for a people and a place to belong, the desire for the freedom and safety you might find there, the thrill and the comfort. Maybe it's what draws you toward the things you hold dear. We often hold on to memories, places, people, and things because there's something of home in them. There's a sense of freedom, the belonging that happens with real friends that makes you feel at home. So many of us are working out a homesickness, and I believe the homesickness is what all our wanderings are all about. We're searching for home—a place of acceptance, a place of fulfillment, and a place of identity. At the basest level, we suspect that home is the place where we'll find our fit, where we'll finally be free.

Rebel

As long as I was with our people—my siblings, my great-grandmother Mama Lois, and our assortment of yard dogs—I rarely teetered on loneliness as a small child. There was an ancient woman across the street named Florence who let us taste her snuff and eat her peppermints. Once in a while, Florence's great-grandchildren would come for summer weekends. When they were gone, I longed for them, for interaction, the connectedness of imaginary play. A neighbor boy from down the road would ride up on his bike when his mama wasn't making him work the garden, and once in a while, Daddy's work friends would bring their children over too. I visited church friends often and came to know myself early as someone who loved to connect with people, to share space and stories.

When kindergarten started, and that big yellow bus picked me up for my thirty-minute ride to school, it was an overwhelming sensory experience. I remember standing in front of my seat as tall as I could and my nose touching the top of the green pleather seat in front of me. I was a tiny thing aching to be seen, looking over. Out the windows were broken-down country roads, then fields of beans and brick homes with paved driveways. I huffed a cloud on the bus window and wrote my name in cursive and remember the honor of the big girl who noticed my swirls. She spoke to me. I remember it as clear as sky above the asphalt plant: "I love your cursive." She saw me.

I remember the gorgeous girl with curly black hair, one shoulder exposed, who sat in the back and sang "Just Another Manic Monday" and "My Sharona" at the top of her lungs. We all loved to hear her sing, especially the boys. She was magnetic brave, wore a bra, and knew how to groove. It didn't take me long to learn her art of connection, the air of sexuality, how it could control things.

After these initial stirrings to connect with the world, to see more than the stretch of yards between home and church, I dabbled in wanderlust every chance I had. I wandered into adolescence and found I could sneak some good MTV time and flip through mountains of romance novels at the house of my great-grandmother Mama Lois. There, I saw Janet Jackson dance. I figured I knew what nasty meant, and I was pretty sure I liked it. I saw the world as a place to be known, a place to connect, to be held in arms.

Even in these early days of budding desire, our Church of Christ youth group had some magical powers and made me feel right enough with God for several years. We memorized the Bible and won Bible Bowl championships. I felt like I belonged as long as I was just like everyone else, and I was able to try for a while. I did my best to keep under the umbrella of God's grace by saying my prayers and no dirty words, wearing long shorts, and vowing never to have sex before marriage. Somewhere along the way, I began to believe that it was my job to make God happy. Somewhere along the way, I believed that making God happy meant conforming to the likeness of a church with all its rules and church programming.

I hesitate a great deal to say a negative thing about the church of my youth, the ones who painted that grace umbrella, the box of faith, for me. They taught me the words to "I'll Fly Away" and "Nearer My God to Thee." They took care of us when Daddy broke his leg, and they surrounded him with love when he lost his oldest sister. They took time off work to be our counselors at camp. I saw Susan Gallant close her eyes when she sang to Jesus. I always watched her because she was different. Once in a while, her palms would turn up. Years later, after I returned to faith, there were renegade women who would confide in me that they had learned it too, that God's consuming love spread far like a thrown net we couldn't get out of. I still don't understand some of their theological arguments, and aren't we all just doing the best we know how?

Back then, in my girl years, I sang "Amazing Grace" with the congregation but felt strangled by guilt, the despair at my pull toward the sensual, at my desire to dance to "Funky Cold Medina." It might have been my own idea that dancing would lead straight away to pregnancy, but it made sense. We were fed a steady diet of works-based, bootstraps righteousness, one that taught us to fear sex, music, and pleasure. Early on, I knew I wasn't good enough. I would never be able to make the

Jesus cut. The Christian requirements seemed simple, but I had too much curious-creative in me not to appreciate art and the body. I didn't know how to not love the skater boys and Cayce Keller with his guitar.

Young as Eve, I thought I knew what gave women power. Oh, the fruit on the tree, it looked good. I knew the long shorts were ugly, and I couldn't not dance to "Motown Philly." I had no place. I thought I would never be able to do enough to be accepted by God's people, and therefore by God. I lived outside the umbrella, and I knew it.

🌿

I lost my virginity in a bedroom while Lenny Kravitz played "Fields of Joy." I was fifteen looking up through the window at the tops of pine trees. We were kissing; his hands moved to my zipper; the word no was inside my mouth. I was a girl. I was a little girl. He was twentysomething, bigger than I. The wind blew the trees until their backs bowed, and I was watching it happen, and I thought I couldn't stop it. I thought I wanted those arms, but this was not a day for being known, not for fields of joy.

When I left his house, a ghost followed me home, the thick presence of something terrible. I went to bed that night and cried until it wasn't dark anymore, that ghost in my room watching me weep. I couldn't get rid of it, but I pressed on and wrote in my journal. "I give up," I wrote, and that was all it took. There, I resolved to a life outside the umbrella. Shame, I know now, was his name.

I woke up to myself, to the mirror like forbidden fruit. I said, "Show me the world." I asked myself, "Isn't there more than these hills? Observe the shape of my lips. See, I'm shaped like a woman." On the scales, I made things add up as best as I could. I plucked my eyebrows, thank goodness, and I became ultimately self-aware. I assumed that I would finally come to freedom in the place I lost it, in the arms of a boy.

Freedom, I thought, was found in the knowledge of good and evil, in tasting both. Isn't that where rebellion begins, when we desire the forbidden thing? For a long span, I lived self-aware, tried to fill my own hollow places. "I'm on my own," I said. It's only me *here*, surrounded by ghosts, eyes opened to the foolishness of trying to please the church. I saw the fruit of sexuality, the art of human connection, and it was good for eating.

Had God pulled me from Adam's rib and placed me naked in the garden, the story would be no different. Let's not blame Eve anymore. If she hadn't eaten the fruit, it would most certainly have been me. I would have eaten it again and again, and then I would have given you a bite.

The fearless leader of my circle of high school friends was Easy. Easy was hard and enlightened and had tattooed in bold print on his wrist the word *freedom*. We all agreed that's what we wanted. We wanted to be free.

In a small town, hardly a soul has grace to spare for the rebellious ones. We would have taken more extreme measures to be different from the rest of the world had it not been so easily done. It was easy to wear funky clothes and stand out, CD case full of Nirvana, Sonic Youth, and the Velvet Underground. It was easy to get pushed to the wayside and easy to be labeled rotten.

When we saw that there was more to the picture, when the institutions became a set of droned rules with which we had no heart connection and the meaning was missing, we rebelled, and we did it with our middle fingers to the sky.

What I remember of that rebellion is that so many of us never had a space to work through difficult circumstances. There was no open culture to discuss pain or injustice. For many families, God was the answer, and he was a God who thought up good youth group T-shirt slogans, who said, "If you just believe hard enough, you'll not suffer anymore."

Look around at the cinder-block houses and the kids whose feet grow holes in their shoes. Look around at the beautiful clothes on the girl whose daddy finds her at night. The God of the bumper stickers doesn't add up here.

We rebellious were trying to find the fix, and most weren't fools for clichéd Christianity, and we good well shouldn't be. So many daddies were gone. Some went home after school to mothers who lay drunk or full of cancer on the couch. One friend woke early before school to chop firewood for money so his siblings could eat.

It was as if one day we all woke up hungry, nearly like zombies. We rose from our parents' houses and said, "None of this stuff feeds us!" We called our parents out. Their faiths seemed hollow, and we wanted free from it.

So many in our community, if they weren't broken and sick outwardly, seemed trite in their outward religion. They wore buns on their heads and sewed their skirts down to the floor. We may have done well to befriend the holiness kids with earnestness, but whether it was true or not, they seemed guilty in being pretty, happy, or fun. Many of us couldn't help but see their "Holy Ghost" as a virus we didn't want to catch.

So we marched, looking for freedom, tasting it together in the bottle, in sex, in circled confession. We made fun of each other and everyone was mean, but there were, too, always arms to cradle. There were long kisses, stories told without judgment. What we didn't have back then was a place to cry. We saw ourselves as broken, like there was no fixing, but there were days we rolled out of school with the windows down. We played our music and waved our arms through the air in the slow ride down to the mill, all the back roads, ghosts in the backseat.

Once I kissed the one who counted stars with me, and after that we didn't leave each other's side. We made promises. We felt so free, watching laughing trees slap their knees because that's what drugs do. They play to your feelings, like music to a dancing baby.

We joined together and watched each other in mutual destruction. In the name of pretty, happy, and fun, we took up a mighty dose of promiscuity and alcoholism. We experimented with every drug and became quite practiced at many of them. I cared so little for my body, all in the name of freedom—as if a lie were being whispered and believed, like death might be the actual secret. Turns out, the harder we fought to show the world that we were well with ourselves, so free, the sicker we became.

All these years later, I wrote Easy and asked him about that tattoo I remember from long ago, and this is how he responded:

I thought I knew why I wanted that tattoo and am glad I have it (for many reasons), but what it meant then and what it means now are from two different continuums. Now, after years of tribulation, turmoil, and personal persecution, I find it has a whole new meaning. Driving along one day I heard a song I had heard a thousand times before and by many different artists, but this one particular day it really hit a nerve with me—a song written by Kris Kristofferson that says, "Freedom's just another word for nothing left to lose," and I realized it is, and that's all it is. Maybe I didn't consciously get that tattoo then for that reason, but that's why I got it in the end. Because when you think about it, "feelin' good" is what it was all about anyway, right?[1]

I think Easy is right. I think it's a long road to the place that says, "I feel good about having nothing to lose." It can be like a trek through the desert to get there sometimes, and that's what it was for me. When my eyes opened, when I chose to put the fruit of the tree of good and evil to my lips, I was beginning my journey into temptation, into chasing the desires that mimic holy freedom. I wish it had taken me only forty days to walk alongside that snake.

All the things offered to me—the freedom, the Turkish delight, the kingdom—I took it all and fed my every desire, and as I did, I heaped up guilt. Guilt, my darling pet, was the one thing I could never seem to lose, and so, freedom really had never been an option for me. Guilt is anti-peace, and without the fruit of peace, there's no real freedom and no real home. Instead, there's only the chasing of other, new desires we hope will fill the hollow.

Capacity: One

Even during my years of rejecting what I had been taught to be true, I would marvel at the fog folding up over the pond. It was the robe of God, the fabric morning unveiling day. It has never been a leap for me to see God in the trees and in the sky. If I saw an eagle shoot up hard like a firework and drop tight like a stone into dark water for a fish, my heart would leap like God might actually know my name. I wondered endlessly at rocks and the coral and shark teeth in caves on the mountain. I wouldn't speak to God, no, but my heart was undergirded with sorrow toward him, how there was always a part of me that knew his kindness existed.

I pursued every desire, thought this kind of freedom would fill me. But this kind of freedom was terribly exhausting, just like all the ways anyone tries to lure love. I kept a boyfriend and a backup. I was the life of the parties. So many of the drugs I used in my teens kept me awake for days. I lied to my parents about everywhere I went and everyone who went with me. There is an entire year I don't remember, only terrifying little flashes here and there.

So many faces have fogged over, memories evaporated, but I do have one clear memory: it was slate gray, wet, 6:00 a.m. at Camp Neyati, time for me to be in the kitchen making eggs and biscuits, setting up trays for the church campers. I hadn't slept at all. I crept down there sliding on pine needles to the edge of the lake where I once saw an otter turn underwater flips. As a little girl, I dug my arm into that same mud unafraid and pulled out crawdads big as lobsters.

The green flash of sun on the bream scales, the black eye, the worm, the hook—all the fear was missing when I came here as a child. That's what I was looking for, I with a hangover at the water's edge. Behind me, Jesus graffiti was splayed on cinder-block basement walls. The mayflies heaved. Blackbirds crackled in the sweet gum tree. Swings creaked. There was no stillness in my heart, but I knew. I was poisoned, and I knew I wasn't alone. I threw a stone at him, and then I went in to work. I believed that all God saw in me were the claws of shame. There was no getting them out.

One year later, I drove in the night with a friend, and the entire left side of my body went numb after a line of cocaine. She was too afraid to take me to the hospital. I know it's a cliché that I shallowly prayed to God, "Save me," but that's the story, like the ones I hear from war. I bargained that if he would save me, I would try to be good like the girls at church. I begged him to make me good. I didn't use cocaine after that, but I couldn't seem to turn my heart around. I was born to be bad, like the bad girls in the movies, like Mallory in *Natural Born Killers*. I was good at it. Even still, I wanted the claws out. I wanted to be loved by God, so I volunteered at camp as a counselor the following summer, because no matter what I was born to be, I had decided to fight hard to be approved by someone who wasn't sick.

I met a boy that summer whose eyes killed me. He prayed with me and asked me to read the Bible. He wrote me long letters, a good boy with the lost girl in Alabama.

Even though I had the most loyal and loving boyfriend, this good boy and his approval of my body and my wayward heart, it undid me. I wanted to marry him. I knew my power. He came to visit me, and we both followed desire to a bed.

With stars in my eyes and a dreamworld up ahead, I became pregnant, and fear strangled me. What I imagined, the lie, was a lifetime cut off from my daddy, an upstanding man with a moral code lined with titanium. If I were pregnant, then my little sister and brothers would be led astray. They would become like me. People would think my family wasn't any good. People would think my church wasn't any good. My precious mama would worry to actual death, and I had already caused enough pain. There had been a fight at church about whether a girl pregnant out of wedlock could be given a baby shower. On top of this, I believed I wasn't good enough or strong enough to be a mama. We could only hope to put the thing behind us with $500.

I was attending a good Christian university, because I hoped the good Christian kids would rub off on me. I acted like life was going better than ever. I enrolled in Bible classes. Wouldn't my daddy be proud? I had a fun roommate who partied enough not to judge my cigarettes. After I unpacked the boxes in my dorm room, I considered my options again. I flipped through the phone book, dialed the number, and a woman told me what time to come.

During the ride, I considered the previous twelve weeks, how I had waffled between tenderly touching my stomach—wanting to hold my baby—and then doing two hundred crunches a day. I had been taking tae kwondo and had become good at meditation. The master would give us a word—strength—and I would visualize, hone in, and manage control of the idea. Strength was to manifest itself physically as I practiced, but everything had moved so far from that. Now, I couldn't will myself from being weak. Only my secrets had muscles that day.

I jittered cold and silent, wanting to curl up in the back. I wanted to scream bloody murder or drive off and get married or jump out of the car as it coasted on the long interstate. But I just sat there shivering, wordless, with my arms straightjacketing my own chest.

The name of the medical building was Freeway. I found the floor and entered where women lined up to be free, so aware of what a baby would do to their lives and what they wouldn't be able to offer a child. I couldn't offer a father or a family at all. I knew what I was.

The room of musical chairs fed into a smaller room with a table. As the nurse called the next person in, we moved down one seat. There was a girl who stood up and ran outside with a change of heart. There were no men in the room that I remember. We were herded in and handed pills to relax us, but I still wept to the point of becoming a spectacle. The nurse chided me and asked, "What's the big deal?" Another girl left her place in line. She was having her third and knew it was hard but right. She gave me her number, said I could call her if I needed to talk after the procedure.

I waffled between becoming an animal in a howl and pulling myself together into a tight numbness. Once in the smaller room, I unclothed myself, put on a light gown, and climbed onto the table. Lying there, I was awake to the sound, relaxed or paralyzed (I cannot tell which) at the hands of the nonchalant man with a mask over his face. The memory muffles it, clouds it over—was it the face of a dog, the mask? He had to work hard. There was a tray, the metal clank, skilled hands at the wheel of a machined eraser. When it was done, I was completely numb, every nerve so doused in pain that shock walked me out, bleeding. I didn't tell a soul about the Freeway Clinic—the free way—how I drained from myself for weeks and weeks after that.

Familiar spirits are real. I was drawn to the ones who struggled in the same ways I did, because an invisible world wooed us together. The spirit with claws in me would nod and smile to the spirit with claws in another. They would whisper across the air and pull me to the ones who had the goods I craved. Familiar spirits tell things about others that no one is supposed to know, and they told me exactly how to present myself. There in Arkansas, I met different versions of the same friends I had back home. I reached out to the beautifully dreaded hippies and planned to smoke weed as soon as possible after my abortion, even there at that Christian school while my life drained invisible right before their eyes. I connected with those who had similarly confused their freedoms, and we went to Memphis on the weekends to get drunk and dance until we couldn't stand.

There has always been something about music and dancing that offers healing or at least a new way to feel the world. In high school, if I were ever able to sneak to a dance, I would come outside of myself, alone on the floor if it had to be that way. I'm not a superb dancer, never had a lesson—just my love, my leg muscles infused with the pulse of stars. Eyes closed, I'm a feeler, a rider, a hearer. I'm a country girl with a body like a connected set of hinges. When I dance, I feel native, home.

That's how it was for me. I would dance to be alone in my grief, to feel something ancient in it. I smiled and worked out the sensuality I had learned as a girl. Showing the underside of a short skirt, yes, those were the saddest days, drunk laughter and dark thud of bass trying to peel me from grief, all the blood still draining out after the *Freeway*.

I went to class and wore grief like a tight lead jacket under my prettiest blouse, and I never said a thing. All my addictions didn't compare to the pain of choosing to erase my first child, that moment on the secret table when I knew it was over. In daily forced chapel, we sang a song about Jesus. I don't remember which song, only that I wept to the point of dry heaving. My lights began to go out, and I neared the end of my own death march, going on like that—drunk, dancing, groping in the dark, draining out for far longer than normal. There was nowhere to go for the screwed-up girls, and the messy ones weren't allowed to stay at this particular Christian university. Sex before marriage was an immediate dismissal.

A month later, the sun blared in on the morning. Present and sick, the taste of alcohol still in my mouth, I walked to the shower. My feet touched the warm patch of linoleum on the floor. Passing the mirror, a girl caught my eye, skinny, pale, dull eyes. I didn't recognize her. I stood and faced myself. The mirror, my idol, she had lied, and I couldn't stand up anymore. I put my hands to the floor and braced like the world would quake open, woozy all the way down to my side in the yellow morning sun. I prayed each breath would be my last. I waited for the tunnel to take me, the blackness to swallow me whole. I planned to wait until it was done. My entire life—the wildcat scream and the laughing trees—it had all led to this.

Giving God an ultimatum is risky, but I had nothing to lose, not anymore, so there on the warm linoleum I said it. "I'm here to die. I fully believe that I will die." And there I gasped my first real breath, as if I'd been swimming up and up from an ear-popping deep. I finally breathed. My body warmed and filled. I drank from the cup from which all metaphors pour. I was Eve again, naked in her garden. When he breathed, my chest rose.

I was trained to argue, but his breath came when I lay with nothing to say, how broken I was. I had nothing with which to entice anyone to come to my rescue. I made no argument and no fight; I wasn't budging in my own power, because I had no power with which to budge. The presence of God, Spirit, warmed my blood and assembled my bones. I crawled to the bed, like one who heard a voice in the desert, saw fire in the bush. A path cleared in me. I whispered, "I am free"—lungs full of air. I was newborn. The weight of legions lifted, taste of forbidden fruit gone from the mouth, sting of death removed. The Bible from class was on the bed, and I drank it like hindmilk. I was broken but filled. The hush in my spirit, this was freedom, the presence of God. Freedom is peace.

The first of many births I would witness was my own. I was born into the light. I would have waited on that linoleum floor until I starved, waited there to be raised from the dead, or be made dead, whichever. I can't explain the difference in what was happening in my head and in my heart and in my body. It was all taking new form. I didn't lie down so that when I stood up I might believe. I lay down to die because I was done with moving about in a body that had no life. The fact that the presence of God was so obvious, like Road-to-Damascus obvious, was absolutely shocking to me. I had never felt so pursued or so loved, and love is what got me up off the floor.

As my eyes came open to something so simple as love, that God loves me, I was overcome with new desire: more than for a warm body—for skin on skin; more than for the taste of home—biscuits and gravy on a family morning; and more than for any drug to numb my pain. I didn't know who I was, filling with such delight, the allure of God. His meeting me on the floor was my release from being bogged down in self-awareness and loathing. He released me from feeling required to entice love, to always make an offering. I became aware of God. He was not only the one who hovered in the fog but also the one who loved me first.

Suddenly, only God was beautiful. Suddenly, I saw through to the unseen, how he stood outside of time for me, and how he sent his Spirit into my time. Suddenly, I had new access to science and law and metamorphosis, the reasons, the metaphors, and the mystery.

I didn't know myself anymore, because I was new. I didn't know what to wear, and so I would ask him. Food tasted different on grateful lips. Three days after I crawled on that floor, I found my cigarettes and threw them in the trash. That's how I quit smoking, how I became found in the only shameless way to lose oneself.

Who was I? I was born a daughter of self-aware Eve in Alabama and then born again through the gospel to freedom, to God awareness. That was the day I stopped pouring out my own blood. I was a whore with liquor on her lips, and now I was Mary Amber, one who kisses Jesus's feet, hair soaked in tears, delighted to be known and desiring only God, and that was enough. God knew my name. He must have been insane, but I went with it. He lavished truth on me. Jesus himself traveled the abyss and through time to meet me on the floor of a dorm room.

I walked with God. That's what Eden was about, man and woman unashamed in the presence of God. That's what was promised to Abraham too—a land flowing with milk and honey, where God would be God in the midst of his people.

When Christ came, when he entered the world into barn air, deep had called into the deep of a woman, and his name was Emmanuel, God with us. It's been the plan all along, the call on every life—we are created beings with the capacity to hold God.

I knew the story—God started with Adam and Eve, breathed life into them both, and called them good. But then desire for the fruit made paths outside of Eden and up into babbling towers. That same Creator God came like breath to me. Like mouth-to-mouth, he breathed in me on a linoleum floor. He called me good. How is it that he chose to grow within young Mary? How is it that he chose to grow within me? God offers himself that way, life in place of death, holy desire replacing deceitful desire, life planted and growing and filling all the hollows of a soul.

I would later learn that Jesus tells us to come to him, all we empty and weary ones.[1] Those of us who can't bear up under the weight of the void any longer, he tells us to come. Come, and he will take our heavy and fill our empty, because he is meek and humble. He gets low down. And when Jesus gets on the floor with you, you will indeed find rest for your soul, a place to belong. If Jesus gets low, then maybe the low way, the broken way of humility, is the best way to be in the peace of his presence, where he whispers in us the direction to a promised land. Maybe the path to Jesus is paved with linoleum.

I learned that Jesus, our God-man, could have considered himself and said, "Look at how ridiculously awesome I am, people. Now worship." But instead he emptied himself, taking on the nature of a servant, obedient to death, not considering equality with God a thing to be grasped.[2] This was my experience, sister to Jesus that I am. I gave up, obedient to death—even death on a linoleum floor—and he roared in. The God of the universe filled me at my very lowest, my emptiest.

Light ruptures dark every time.

Becoming Kin

Let him kiss me with the kisses of his mouth.

Song of Solomon 1:2

If anyone had really known me, no one would have taken me in. That's what I believed. I was a nameless, unrecognizable girl with hardly the gumption even to wander around trying to find a place to land. But the day God got on the floor with me was the day he claimed me. I was named, and I was learning what it meant to be home. Often when a child is adopted, right away she has a home and a name, but sometimes it can take a while before she feels taken in, a long time before she feels known.

There will always be ways I'm learning to let God love me, but maybe I inherited more than desire for the knowledge of good and evil from our Eve. Maybe I inherited her memory, the echoes of the garden. There was the faint memory of the cadence of his walk in the cool of the evening. There was the settled stride I remembered. Oh yes, I remembered that he had seen my freshest skin. He had seen my naked heart. There was a memory in my spirit that he had called me beloved. His smiling on me was always his original intention.

In these new memories, I recognized his gentleness with me, a girl child from Alabama with mud in her fingernails. I recognized an invitation to be satisfied, even to be naked before him. There was a time when shame had no place in my life, like with Eve before the fruit, and there in the beginning of faith, I remembered it well. I lived it. No shame.

I saw this potential for others also. I knew God was everywhere and knew there were glimpses of him in all people, because he showed me his kindness and his mercy in all creation. Even in the great sin and shame of others, I saw him, or at least I saw the groaning for him. In this, I learned to recognize the hollow, the search for God, and the deep longing for him (for fulfillment) in the needles, the skin, and the bottle. I recognized his wooings in every metaphor. I saw the desire of skin on skin as the soul looking for home, for intimacy. I saw the body, made for God, as an original intention, as a belonging.

Our lives are made of metaphor, and we can recognize Jesus throughout creation and in those who have never heard his name. The apostle Paul wrote in Romans 1 that no one has an excuse. God is everywhere. Yoga poses and Gregorian chant, buttermilk cornbread, the Grand Canyon, and the picture of a rainbow drawn by the hand of my two-year-old all speak of him if we're looking. Don't make a mistake and hear that I worship those things; no, instead I worship the God of the universe who *is*. "For from him and through him and to him are all things. To him be glory forever! Amen."[1] His scent wafts through tent cities, jail cells, granite kitchens, and marble palaces. He beckons us in all places. Where can I go from him? The echo of him in metaphor throughout the earth is undeniable when one wakes to him.

When I first believed, I walked around in a clumsy prayer, so awake, listening for God in the falling of an acorn, in everything. I was free to lapse into long spiritual metaphor simply by hearing my alarm clock. Some might accuse me of being led purely by emotion. Let it be so. It was the feeling of love, of very first love. Let it also be understood that I studied Scripture like a brain on steroids. I studied homiletics. It was a mind transformation, a decision as best as one knows how to make in the midst of being overcome. I was ridiculous really, and I didn't need cigarettes or anything else—not a cute tush, no nightlong blitzes, and certainly not a fella to keep me company.

I didn't have the language for it then, but I saw the Imago Dei everywhere and in everyone. I saw myself as a child of God, Abba letting me come to him, boldly and with ease, in the gentleness of relationship. I was confident, and I saw God as one who loved me completely as a good Father. And Jesus—he, my love, my brother—became my friend. He was becoming the only place that made any sense to me, the only way to see the world.

❧

I decided to join a club called Ju Go Ju—the Christian university equivalent to a sorority. I couldn't believe it either, but I felt compelled to make friends with other people who followed Jesus. The girls made me wear a lame bow in my hair like they did, but the girls were nice, and I was a new thing, a little hippie lamb learning to fit with the practiced Christians, so it was peachy at the time. The conformity to that social club was a miniature training ground for how to be a part of the church structure. Ju Go Ju is how I dipped my toes into group think.

We were at the student union, and everyone flocked like gulls on fresh bread to some tall, shiny-haired guy. I normally would have been too cool to bend my neck, but alas, I had to get all the Ju Go Ju beaus to sign a sheet of paper as a part of my initiation into the club, and I heard this one was a beau. What is a beau? Simply, a beau of a social club is one of the cute guys that the girls voted worthy to be allowed to hang out with them at all times; they are the equivalent to Christian guy groupies. I'll admit it: the entire thing was just plain weird.

Seth was cheery and wore a soft, frayed Polo shirt. He had a firm handshake and was confident. He did not seem mysterious or at all like he would ponder endlessly in dark corners. I stood there, staring, and he walked straight to me, and this was our conversation:

> Hi. My name is Seth.
> Oh. Hi. I'm Amber.
> Where are you from?
> Alabama.
> Are you an Alabama fan or an Auburn fan?
> Uh. I don't care. I don't watch football.
> Okay. Well, nice to meet you.
> Yeah. You too.

It certainly wasn't romantic—hardly anything to note. I picked up my things and scooted to the other side of the room to study. As I read through notes, I was drawn to watch him. I couldn't stop. The more I looked (and I tried not to) and the more I prayed, the more I developed a full-on crush. It happened within seconds that God gave me the news, and I thought, *Yeah, it would be crazy if he were the one I'm to marry.*

Back then, though, when I had first been born into that believing heart, I felt encased and protected. I was completely secure. I told God that he could pair us if he wanted, and then I stood back—except for this one night before church when I wondered if it was the same place Seth would worship. I spent a while in front of the mirror that night. I put myself together as if Seth would be there, and when I arrived and found my seat, I felt guilty. The congregation sang, and I realized I was going to church for the sole purpose of landing myself a mighty good-looking man. I was sorry at the thought. I prayed about it, and God loved me, so I sang to him.

And behind me started a voice, one unique and beautiful voice. I looked over my shoulder. Seth was singing—unconcerned with me—and, let me tell you, he was strong on handsome.

We talked after the service. He left for a week, and when he returned, he came straight to my dormitory and called me from the phone in the lobby. I ran down the hall in a baggy sweater, torn jeans, and my sock feet. We had thirty-five minutes before curfew, and we took it over coffee. We took it with nonstop story. From that very first moment, we didn't know how to hold back anything. I told him every secret, about the abortion and my addictions. We took every spare minute either of us had after that, and we both knew.

A month later, over Thanksgiving break, he bought my ring, and over Christmas break, he proposed. I had known him for two months, but I would have said yes after two weeks. During this time, I laughed uncontrollably even while alone. We were every cliché and everything new—all trust and rest and wide-open love. This is the beginning of our love story. I don't recommend others follow our example, but I've learned that there aren't many rules to this love thing, so, fine, go ahead.

Seth was a virgin and always said, even out loud, that he would marry a virgin, which is funny because I can't say we made it to our wedding day, even though we strapped on every rule we could to keep us pure. The rules we already knew weren't working, so we added some extras like, "Don't go parking at night on a dead-end street," for example. Oh, but our hearts were burning. Seth was a youth minister in training, and I was a fresh Jesus girl whose jeans had the shape of a cigarette box still worn into the back pocket.

In that early stage, steam rose up as we tangled our arms together, leaning in for a walk. We whispered as we walked to a dark station. My lips hovered hot at his ear. One night, where the old, empty freights lined up next to the track, we climbed in one, and as we began to kiss, an eighteen-wheeler from nowhere slung into our pitch black, straight out of a horror movie, the driver flashing his lights and pulling his horn, and he jumped out yelling and running before his wheels stopped. Neither of us had ever had to run so fast down a set of tracks, our hearts already banging in our chests.

In this early love, I didn't need to sleep and I wasn't hungry. Chocolate had no taste. If you were my teenage daughter, I'd call it lust, but there was a bigger metaphor at work in us, and the forces of intimate love are strong. Oh, the tug of war between rebellion and freedom—when it comes to sex, it has been the hardest thing to maneuver. We were consumed with desire for each other and ready so early.

Before the train station was the drive to a concert. The hole ripped in the knee of my jeans was wide, and he was able to stick his finger in and touch the back of my knee. There, a key turned, the curtain pulled way back, the lights came on, and a river sprang up. The first time his skin touched my skin, I was blind for minutes, while internal wires shot off all wildly exposed, awake, and setting fire. All he had done was touch my leg! I remember seeing his arms for the first time. This is ridiculous. It's not like I hadn't seen a man's arm before, but with Seth, it didn't matter. I loved everything about him—his arms, his Bible, and the passenger seat of his little black car.

There are certain seasons of life that offer sudden and strong shifts in identity. These shifts send one into a liminal space, a threshold between identities. We were in between, the realm between fleshly desire and the holy.

When we first fell in love, it was all open. We were lost in the joy of it. Our mouths were perfect together. We were on the threshold where previous understandings and molds are broken in order for us to transition into our new roles, new identities

in marriage. The threshold of young love, right before marriage, is a tricky time, and some people transition very well. I
was not one of them.

Lust used to be the driving force, a chance for relief somehow,
but when I met Seth, how was our strong desire to be skin on
skin not holy all along? We had restraint, and that restraint was
good, because we wanted to deem our marriage as set apart.
Even still, those wild feelings weren't from Satan. They weren't
dirty. They were the desire to be naked with a man before God.
They were a desire to live our Edenic memories, to be Adam
and Eve before the fruit of self-awareness touched their lips.

Something happens in the erotic love meant to mirror the
freedom believers receive in Christ. The metaphor of two becoming one—the intimacy in union, the freedom of expression and pleasure therein—is given as a metaphor for Christ
and his bride. Now, I honestly have a hard time wrapping my
mind around sex with God, but I don't have trouble coming
back to the idea of nakedness before him, about being exposed
and the desire to be completely known. As with Adam and Eve
in the garden, I am most free when I am walking unashamed,
unafraid, and wide open.

Sex gives us a little Eden back, a small flash in the mirror of
when our kind walked with God. A metaphor is never wasted.
He knew what he was doing when he blew breath into dust.
Often we Christians could learn something from the addicts,
how to go hard after God. Addicts are going for it again and
again, the mimicry of freedom in an oxytocin rush, the calm,
the belonging, the temporary fit. The rush of oxytocin is the
beautiful science of God, flooding us with a bonding hormone

that initiates feelings of safety, empathy, and pleasure. When we are skin on skin, oxytocin aids in healing processes and in stress relief.

I experienced a lot of perceived sexual freedom before marriage, and I do know how rebellious it sounds for me to say any good lesson might be learned through fornication, and yes, I had plenty wrong then. It would have been nice if I had waited, if I had learned it in marriage, but I didn't. Even in this, there are notes of redemption, flashes of beauty and freedom.

At our rehearsal dinner, we ate gumbo flown up from New Orleans, and Seth's Louisiana family toasted our love. Our wedding day was in an Alabama November, and the maples in the churchyard were fire red. My gown was stark white, and when the doors opened, I entered in holding my daddy's arm. Drums played, and Seth cried.

We honeymooned one night with a view of the lake, and the next day we drove through Arkansas. We stayed in a bed and breakfast, ate apple soup, and sneaked tiny sips of sherry before we drove to Tulsa to be good Baptist grown-ups.

My young, free body was meant for Seth's, yet when I married him and fell under what was supposed to be holy, I got all jangled up about it. There's nothing like pulling into the megachurch office building where your new husband works with God-fearing men in stiff suits to set the mood only two days after getting married. Now, I was to attend church in upstanding sweater sets and lead a youth group. Sex was good when it was dirty, and I liked it a lot before I got married, but now I was clean. Suddenly, I was squeaky clean, but I didn't know how to act that way. Within days, I switched from being naked and unashamed in intimacy to being self-studying so that I could be found good enough to keep. Sex again became a tool, this time for wooing my own husband, and I couldn't get it right because I was still carrying the shame of being dirty.

I know now that what I had believed to be dirty as a young one wasn't dirty at all. No matter how temporary the relationship, I should have carried what I learned from sex before marriage straight into marriage. I should have known to continue looking for freedom, the kind of freedom that brings life, reflections even of life eternal.

In my younger years, I had learned the mimicked version. There was shame, yes, but there was also what drew me to the mimicry, the nakedness, two people in self-expression with one another. The shame weighed down heavily then, but there were reprieves. There was good love in my youth, and I don't deny that I shared sacred moments with other men. What I experienced was a loss of self-awareness, which happens to be very good for someone running from herself. I learned to throw self-consciousness down in the pile on the floor with my clothes.

The truth is we were created to be sexual beings. Unfortunately, I learned a little more than how to lose myself, how to shed inhibitions. I learned to use sex, like the women in the books, as a way to control and to pursue intimacy. I feigned maturity and found it a source of power. The metaphor of sex for me was sullied by so many nuances that I certainly didn't understand it at the time.

And now here we were, two young married children, and the gift of sex with my husband provided us with a beautiful, new, multidimensional metaphor for freedom. We literally puzzle-pieced together. We fit, and we didn't care the shape we were in. There was the deep longing for closer and closer until we were finally, literally flooded with release. I read about this biblical metaphor, but that's exactly how it remained. We didn't understand intimacy because shame is directly opposed to it.

Before our wedding day, my daddy told me that "when you first marry, you love him, but you don't share blood with him. Only certain things can make your blood one and the same. You can have a husband, but it takes a while to become kin."

When Seth and I first married, after the weekend honeymoon our church allowed, we were not at home. Seth worked for that church, and Oklahoma was strange for me. I only said "home" in reference to Alabama, where folks would grab you by the shoulders after church and say, "The sweet tea's made, and we've got a roast on. Y'all are eating lunch with us."

Our apartment was a terrible mess. If you twitched big, you might accidentally end up in another room. We fought once because I didn't give him a receipt for a Snickers Bar. I had medical bills, and Seth had to sell a guitar. We counted a ninety-hour workweek and figured he made about $0.95 an hour. We thought we could make a better home if we just had more money, so Seth started writing music and traveling to lead worship, and I mostly enjoyed staying alone, skipping church, and treating myself to candy bars, but it wasn't until his trip to Mexico that I felt it.

Being kindred means you come from the same people, and though he said "prawlines," and I said "praylines," I hadn't recognized it in him until he had been gone for twenty-one days. The church bus pulled into Houston after winding out of the mountains and crossing the border, and he called me, and I sat in the living room for the entire rest of that day. I waited. I fumbled with the remote. I stared at the birdless skinny limbs off the balcony. It turned a long, moonless dark.

He walked in and put his bags on the floor. He came to the place where I had waited all day, and we didn't talk till the morning. It wasn't the wedding night that we crossed over. The self-awareness I had mustered in my fear of not belonging broke down in my adoration of him. He was my kindred, and when he was finally home, I was finally home too.

On the brink of some tough things, we still had so much good, so much that God was doing and pulling together. There was such a strong and positive process of redemption that churned within us, even if our moments of kinship felt few.

A Harness
on the Wind

The wind blows where it wishes, and you hear its sound, but
you do not know where it comes from or where it goes. So
it is with everyone who is born of the Spirit.

John 3:8 ESV

We meandered skinny, county roads nearly four hours to get
there, but up in Tennessee was half my family, seventeen first
cousins and my daddy's mama, who we called Mamaw. When
we turned down her long, chert road, there were woods dotted
with newspaper-lined structures, old hideouts and houses with
rotting shoes beneath the composting leaves. This is the native
land. This is the land torn by Confederate and Union, blood and
the running from blood. To the right was a field centered with a
tall, gnarly tree that silhouetted the sky. It was the haunted tree,

the skeleton of a life before, and once in a while, it swarmed with bees. There was always a sense that Mamaw's road had a blackness to it, the sweetness of honey within. The road was a portal to yesterday, the old way of farming, a blacksmith shop, the mule attachments, and the old pots pulled from a house that had burned to the ground. There was history in the air and an attic there, too, where lived secrets along with our own imagined lore of "rawhide and bloody bones," a Cherokee ghost out for vengeance. The quilts were stacked up there—pieced-together, ancient fabrics—so soft and frayed that the batting poked through.

Behind Mamaw's house were acres for roaming. My cousin Philip climbed oak trees like ladders, and I followed. Arrow-heads and pieces of pottery were everyday treasures. Kids were everywhere. I still have scars from pushing through barbed wire, ignoring pain for possible adventure. Woven walls of saw briars mangled the way to old swimming holes and copperhead dens. There was danger, yes, and there were stories we knew we could never hear, but above it all was Mamaw and Aunt Josie both saying, "I love you, baby."

Worn rocks trailed up to the front porch, where plants dangled and dripped with fresh water. Mamaw's plants were always green, aloe vera always ready to break for the healing. Hear the creak of a porch swing, the echo of a family gathered to sing a cappella hymns, always the hum of nature; Mamaw's house was alive with the sounds and smells of love and welcome. She loved me before I learned to make people think I was beautiful. She loved me before I knew who I was. She loved me when I was small.

I never stopped wanting to be under Mamaw's roof. Even in the worst of my rebellion, she would take me in and mention nothing of danger. She loved me in. It was a regular thing for her to have something boiling, coffee spitting in a percolator or pot, cast iron browning something up. Her house was the house where I slept the best. If only while there, her house kept me from a damaging lifestyle. Once I woke there in the flat heat of a summer night. I was in the iron bed right next to the open window. I heard so many feet through the grass, the coyotes running in a howling pack. She was the one who kept a box fan in the window, between me and the dogs.

We knew nothing of priesthood there, but Mamaw must have splattered cooking oil out the doors in the chicken scraps. She had the strength of one anointed, one who could claim you. She kept the shame out. It would snarl at the door, but inside was safe. Maybe that's why we rebellious ones always clung to her. She wasn't our favorite because she was lenient toward us. She was our favorite because she was a reprieve. There was something of the rest of Eden in there, something of my Jesus.

Mamaw came from and married into a family with a long sense of self and survival. Her daddy was a World War I soldier muddied up in trenches who kept a silk hankie in his pocket that belonged to her mama. She lost her first love and a nephew in war, and her oldest son fought in Vietnam. There was a Cherokee daddy and a Cherokee mama hiding in there at different times, and then there was the Hurst family way back, whose stories are just as good as the Hatfields'. My fifth great-grandfather was in the militia who fought in the Battle of King's Mountain in the Revolutionary War, but Mamaw's way wasn't the gun like the rest, though she could ring a neck if she needed to. She knew how to make a skillet of cornbread to keep life going at the table. She was a revolutionary too. We come from a long line of them. I know where I come from. My blood is always telling me to stand for something.

She didn't mean to teach me that Jesus was one who worked in scraps or one who took on strays, but she did. She taught me what the church is supposed to look like. She took care of what she had. She gave part of it away. Then she didn't worry about the rest, especially about what she looked like or how she was perceived. Half my life, her house didn't even have an underpinning. It wasn't her job to make the world beautiful. All she did was feed us and give us a place to rest.

When I first believed, I stood for a Spirit who roamed low on floors, though I hardly had language for it. I didn't know to be held back about it. I was as restrained as the ear-chopping Peter ever dreamed of being. I would read and read the Bible and then go tell it on the mountain with whatever words I could pull together. I had the passion of a thousand fires singing, "Grace, grace, grace." It was a new revolution for me.

It didn't take me long to see how different I was in the church. Right before we got married, I was fresh in the memory of wild back roads. I was fevered with a rescuing when we visited the mega-ginormous church building where Seth was employed. It was the Fourth of July service, and that thing was everything but indoor fireworks. People marched down three aisles waving flags from all the states, and the choir was bellowing some serious worship music to our great country. It was a spectacular show complete with brain-jarring organ music piping through every wall.

Every church service was my giving in a little more, a little water on my flame, revolution being tamed with every outline I made. I tried my best to dull my senses to it, because everyone acted like our youth group rules were normal, and I was determined to love them, ready to finally have my part in the church. I was ready to receive it with an open heart, even though I had walked in there like a throbbing sore thumb.

I made a mistake when I came into the church. I walked in newly transformed, with a diamond on my finger, and I asked them, "Will you love me now?" If I change the way I dress, calm down some, use your language, and learn to defend the faith well, if I accept the parades of the church and all the fancy fireworks, will you love me then?

All my motives switched into a begging for the church's love. I hated the organ, but I had imagined that the church would love me how my mamaw had. We would see revolution together and show the world a great peace. Once I aimed for that kind of acceptance, I didn't burn so much for my first love anymore. Instead, I joined the regime, the open arms of the big, pretty machine. Pastor Black would preach, and I would nod in agreement, but a scream perched at the edge of my mouth. I had to get control of it. Most days I thought I would drown. I was terrified of losing the church's love and my own fresh goodness.

I had no idea how to reconcile the holy, wild Spirit who had rewritten me from within with how holy and ironed we were trying to look on the outside. The church was so tidy and clean, so aware of how it looked, that I kept my focus on what to wear and how to sound when I sang. I had a lilac sweater set and matching eye shadow. My smile and my body were beautiful. I offered myself up to the church.

The way I understood it, no one suffered in this church, except maybe from physical sickness. No one talked about brokenness or the poor unless it was to mention how someone else wasn't doing well: *so sad*. I did my best to look good enough for the keeping, but my secrets weighed me down, how broken I was and how I didn't fit. I bore within me the consequences of my own wrongdoing. Right at the surface level, I ached with longing. My arms were empty. I was a childless mother, and not a soul knew. I was a year removed from snorting cocaine off a stranger's bathroom countertop and missed my broken friends from home so desperately. I had left them. I had left the dorm room floor. I had left home, a turncoat in a lilac sweater and a smile.

We made so little money then that I got a job at the Clinique counter wearing a white lab coat. I sold makeup and learned to make others feel more beautiful. After skipping a few Sundays at church to work, I was corrected by the staff because of how it might look.

I knew I would figure it out eventually. I knew if I tried hard enough I would wrangle back at grief's own throat. It seemed the rest of the church had done it, had healed up good. It was either that or no one knew how to grieve at all. In church work, you hear the stories, the rumbles of despair, divorce, drugs, but I never once heard a public admission or any cries for help. Had I told someone that I was broken, I'm not sure what would have happened. Instead of aiming for confession and true reconciliation within the church, I adored her models and how clean she looked. I was learning to control my own grief, conforming into the likeness of the church.

Once in a while, I would shower and weep. I wore tears soaked into my hair. I was afraid they would find me out, that they would find out about my abortion. I was married. I was twenty-one. I was afraid they would all find out I was a fake or that I might stand up and call everyone there fake. I was a preacher inside burning, trying to die to parts of my own story and wanting to run away from who God was making me. I was constantly threatening to bloom into a prophet, like one wearing too much perfume. Nothing about me felt allowed.

We told the kids in our youth group not to listen to secular music. That left them with terrible Christian music from the nineties. I was one of them, fearing the pit, the devil crouching, and I hated that music. I constantly shifted the fear and hate to keep the grief from showing. We were youth group leaders trying to unify ourselves to the church so we could prove we were the people of Jesus. But I had actually left my people behind.

My people were the ones underground. Mine were the ones turning animal on drugs, voodoo kids made of moonshine and casserole, the trailer and the weed. We knew where we came from: broken earth, dead ends, dirty river water. I would sneak out windows at night to be with my people. Doing so was more important than sleep. Coming into the church was like stepping on the inside of a different cage at the zoo. Oh, I couldn't tell which exhausted animal I was anymore, one not much different than the other.

I was becoming a different sort of self-aware, watching myself closely to find freedom through conformity. It seems I would have leaned left. It seems I would have wanted to stay out of the box, but I desperately craved to be on the inside. Everyone looked the same, so I took that to mean it was true unity, the body acting like Jesus. I did as they did, and I learned to do it better. I thought the homogeneity of the church was the answer to my grief.

There are five simple points to Calvinism, and I decided that I liked that. I understood that there were people created for glory and people created for destruction. I wasn't sure which I was. What about my friends back home? Raging inside, I soothed myself with the system. I suckled at outlines, every black-and-white answer a pleasure that fit like a key into an opiate receptor. I was systemizing it all: the fall, sin, poor Job, creation, art, free will, and election. I was trying to fit within the unified body, signaling *love me more love me more love me more.*

We said with our mouths that we were of a New Covenant, of no law, but we imposed guidelines so meticulously that you couldn't squeak out a hug without feeling guilty. Seth and I laid out rules for the youth; we called a hug that was too close "hunt-frugging," and it wasn't allowed outside of marriage. There was a rule for everything so no one would have leeway to hear the Spirit incorrectly. In fact, you could only hear the Spirit by learning how the church understood Scripture. We were always on guard, asking ourselves, "What if we end up like the Holy Rollers? What if the youth group speaks in a tongue we don't understand? What if they start teaching that you must do something to earn your salvation?" We made rules to keep people from making rules. Our efforts to tame ourselves were desperate.

⚜

Back then I still had my mamaw. She would talk to me on the phone, and when I came over, she rocked in her chair. She told me secrets. We became so close in our brokenness that we spoke in secret language during the days before she slipped away from cancer into her real life. Her own confessions unified us, and her perfect love for me cast out fear.

What I sensed from the church was that perfect love adopts fear. So much hammered doctrine was an effort to control, as if it were our own job to uphold the morality standards of Jesus for the world, rather than to be embodied by the actual Spirit of the living God. We used doctrine to harness the Holy Spirit, just in case it got rowdy, just in case something happened that we couldn't explain or in case it asked us to do something we didn't want to do. We used doctrine and codes so we could feel better about ourselves. If something is outlined and explainable, then we can size ourselves up and see how well others are doing too. Doctrine, how we laid out our knowledge, became a measuring stick that we superimposed into the very hand of God. Doctrine became God.

I love to learn. I know it's true that lovers of learning have only God's character to gain when in the Spirit, and even Scripture teaches, "For one person is given through the Spirit the message of wisdom, and another the message of knowledge according to the same Spirit."[1] Knowledge is a gift of the Spirit and helps me connect the dots of my own life to the biblical narrative, but when knowledge twists inward and puffs up the hollow places with self-consumed pride, we begin to break down. Love is what builds us up,[2] but I was breaking down.

I see now that using any doctrine like a harness to keep a moral upper hand on the world is corrupt. Jesus didn't come to modify the behavior of the church. He came to set her free. He came to be the way straight to the mercy seat of God. He didn't come to bring us the Bible, though that's often how we live. He came to establish a kingdom and his righteousness by his own Spirit in our transformed lives. Too often we're prone to worship the Good Book, as perfectly true as those words may be.

These days, I hold the Bible in the mornings, and the crinkle of the pages makes me glad. I read, and I cry. I believe. Phrases trigger questions that bleed into my journal. I ask. I seek. I knock. But I do not believe the Bible is a fourth person of the Trinity.

"In the beginning was the Word, and the Word was with God, and the Word was God."[3] I'm not sure we're able to see this verse but through a mirror dimly, but I don't think at creation God was holding the Bible. I believe he was with himself as Trinity: the Father, Son, and Holy Ghost. "The Word became flesh and dwelt among us."[4] The Word was Jesus, and as Jesus ascended into heaven to sit at the right hand of God, he told us, "Now I will send the Holy Spirit, just as my Father promised. But stay here in the city until the Holy Spirit comes and fills you with power from heaven."[5] I wish I had learned this in the infancy of belief.

I leaned so heavily on doctrine that I turned away from belief that the Holy Spirit was active anywhere other than in the reading of Scripture. I was afraid. I was afraid of the Holy Spirit for so many reasons, not to mention the fear of being associated with the pew hoppers and faith healers of our charismatic city—much less the snake handlers of my Appalachian roots. I thought I could measure him or steer him. I thought five solas could contain him. I thought fear might help me fit in.

There were clearly defined ways to be "godly," but these were devoid of the Spirit of God, and I didn't give any allowance to his leading from within. What is Scripture if it doesn't pour in, transform, and then flow out from the depths, especially as love, not only as love for others but also as love for the self? After all, the second commandment after love God is that we love others as we love ourselves.[6]

The self for me to love was broken, and the church around me was not. So instead of loving myself in that brokenness, instead of sticking out like a sore thumb, I took on the original meaning of shame and tried to cover up. I dried my face and painted it. I whitewashed my story and lived like beauty was the point, to be unbroken.

There came a time for me in that first year of marriage in that tiny apartment when I began to loathe myself, the farce, and self-loathing makes a marriage sick. I believed again the shame heaped on me like heavy, old garments I was meant to wear. No matter how much I adored Seth, my shame held him at arm's length. I found myself, again, unable to add up to the righteousness required of me. This is what codes do; they show you your shortcomings. That was the exact purpose of the old Jewish law, and it's the purpose of our codes today. As I helped make boundaries for the youth group to keep them from sinning, without any mention of the Spirit or Imago Dei, the weight of my own sin fell on me hard. I believed my record had been forgiven, but I relapsed into shame. Shame wrings the life from belief.

Shame is an addictive drug that hunts you down. There's always someone around every corner who's going to offer you the opportunity to pick it back up. I didn't know I could let it back in, but when I took off my clothes, I couldn't bear to be naked with my own husband. Once, I cried instead and wondered if I missed old boyfriends. I wondered if I had made a mistake. I wondered if maybe I wasn't cut out for Jesus or Seth either. Shame is a powerful and confusing drug.

I knew exactly what to do about it too. I would find my theology. There it is: the depravity of man. It was easy for me to accept that doctrine! Oh, I loved it. My filthy-rag status was at the front of my mind, which can be freeing at first, because it's wonderful to hear that I can do nothing to earn God's love, especially since I got his attention by crawling drunk on the floor. But the depravity of man became my darkest trap, a sort of living purgatory where I reveled in my inabilities, believing I had earned my own emptiness. "There is no one who does good, not even one."[7]

I became paralyzed and self-consumed.

Realizing our inability to earn righteousness isn't meant to be a rat wheel to run on. The depravity of man is only the realization of the hollow, the need. Depravity should only imply that we can be filled with God. I wish I had known.

If I had known the Spirit really existed, other than to speak to men on what to write in ancient scrolls; if I had known I could walk in the Spirit, like someone not addicted to a body; if I had known the Spirit crawls on floors and meets in the underside, I would have listened closer to the winds as they came through. There were moments I knew he was there—the water's edge, how the whip-poor-will called us home, how my mamaw loved me. There were moments with Seth when our love came back to me, glimpses of our kinship.

Our systemized theology was our way to harness the wind, to get some reins on the Holy Spirit so we could manipulate him to the left or the right. Our systemized theology was a way to fit, to assimilate, and that was my desire—to fit into a people. But there was never anything so exhausting as that, as acting like we could control God, as trying to fit into a people who believed they could control God. I was running out of energy, looking to fill the empty hollow again. Too self-aware and anemic, I let go of the reins. Isn't it sometimes God's mercy that we crash?

Hungry

If you want to keep me, treat me like a child before bedtime. Invite me to your story time or to hear your poetry read aloud. Sit up in a chair and let the room go quiet. Give it pause. Let the space hang. Let me sit on the floor, leaning back on my elbows, poking my legs out straight and wobbling side to side. Crack a book open, lick your finger, and let me hear the page. Read in rhythm. Use your narrator voice, crescendo. Sing a song and I'll become unaware of my body, my mouth hanging open as I go with you. I am always hungry for this, for a story to swallow me whole.

The stories, the rhythms, they remind me of my childhood. So many of my cravings are like this, a beckoning back to an innocent Eden, my childhood where my daddy never stopped telling stories. He never stopped pointing out the stars, how they sing. He made our lives better than fiction. Our bedtime stories were a series about small creatures who lived in our woods named Yimlets. I learned imagination and song from him.

He played guitar or banjo, and my sister and I would dance. Those Appalachian songs told stories of love and heartache. We got the love of music from Daddy. Under the covers at night, after he said good night, I would turn the radio down as low as it could go and press record on the tape player when a good song came on. My bedroom window was long, and when it turned dark, I could see myself in the reflection, like a full-length mirror with the whole world on the other side. I danced to myself, even under the covers. I learned the way of toe tapping, of beats on a set of hips, how shoulders talk without lips. I can't help but dance, to have bass pull me up like on marionette strings. What music or storytelling was in Eden, I don't know, but I guarantee it was there.

Some mornings, after breakfast, I followed my daddy. All I knew was to follow him. He had a machete and would go ahead of me until we got to the muscadines. It felt like fiction to find wild grapes hidden there in such black, dangling bunches. Sometimes I am hungry for the rhythm of boots through brush, the dust, the tougher skin, and the sweet burst of wild in a grape.

When the heart longs for community in story or music, when it longs for pleasant memory and taste, and when we want expression in art of motion, to move on from where we are, what are we to do? What are we to do with desire? "Each person is tempted when he is lured and enticed by his own desire. Then desire when it has conceived gives birth to sin, and sin when it is fully grown brings forth death."[1]

Even in the Eden of my girlhood, I was taught that desire led to death. So in my new faith, rather than give in to desire, fall into sin, and die, I decided to kill off desire instead. This is what I thought church was for. I lay down before her—the church—like I had on the dorm room floor. I waited for passions to die. I waited to feel alive. Even as I was ingesting Scripture like it was water to guzzle for the fires of desires within, I felt that I was losing my life and my strength. If you were to ask Seth why we left that mega-church in Tulsa, he'd have a different answer that had much to do with politics and money, the shady ways of church gone high-minded and business savvy. But for me, I just left tired of wrestling desire. Church couldn't help me with it anymore.

That drunk morning on the dorm room floor kept coming back to me again and again. That first morning of belief, when I stood at a mirror and didn't recognize the girl staring back at me, I was skin and bones. I didn't think I would ever do without the food offered to me that day. Entering into faith was coming into the promise of manna, satisfaction available at the turn of every new day. "Come and eat," Jesus is always saying.[2]

Instead of being Christ's image bearers, those in likeness to Jesus, offering real nourishment in Spirit, the regimented church was a copycat version of Christianity.

We had put our hope in an imposter, and it left us full of cravings. No matter how much I read the Bible, I didn't know who I was anymore or how to feel alive. I sure didn't hear Jesus calling my name; there was no "come and eat." Looking to church doctrine for continued salvation and approval sent me into starvation mode. My gaze zoomed inward in constant evaluation, either in condemnation or in congratulations. Such self-awareness creates a black hole of a heart. I became void, disconnected, and hungry, and when you're hungry, you always go looking for food until you think you've found it.

We left Tulsa and moved to Fayetteville, where the hills roll green up into mountains covered in laurel and dogwood. Fayetteville, Arkansas, is a strange town with a twist of academic and hippie, Bible Belt and Wiccan, quiet faith and picket line. They pride themselves in the market on the square where you can hear their boys on the banjo, the girls clapping, the women playing upright bass. Fayetteville in the summer is for peaches, blooms, and handmade soaps. The girls wore tank tops, tattoos, and long skirts, so immediately it felt like home to me, like glory, like crawling out of winter concrete straight into a garden of happy.

Grandma and Grandpa Haines lived there right in the center of town on a piece of land in an Ozark stone house built in 1937. We called it the Rock House. It smelled like Dr Pepper, silver polish, and china cabinets in there. It smelled old, like a home that had been home before you knew it existed. The attic was lined with boxes of business records to prove success and boxes of felt cutouts for forty-year-old Sunday school lesson boards. Then there were boxes of teacups and dessert plates for hosting church gatherings. It was the home place and a collection place for multiple generations. Grandma moved in there with her parents and planted yellow roses by the koi pond during World War II while Grandpa was in Italy. When I spent the night with them, I slept in the room with the displayed knife, gun, sack, and badges of a Nazi. There was also a human skull, but let's not talk about it.

Behind the Rock House was a tiny white house with two bedrooms built for Grandma's grandmother. We called it the Love Shack. We lived there for $325 a month and ate ice cream with Grandma and Grandpa every night during *Wheel of Fortune*. I picked bouquets of yellow roses, peonies, lilacs, and tulips from the property. I overdecorated with picture frames and used fabric to cover old furniture we had found in the chicken house.

The chicken house was half fallen in and full of boxes and rotting furniture. It was proof of the depression era, after which nothing could be discarded. There were jars of elastic from old waistbands, jars of ripped stockings, and jars of rusty nails. There were swimming pools and Christmas trees and trunks full of moldy *Penthouse* magazines. The family never threw anything away, but everything that needed to be hidden went to the chicken house. It all waited there to be reclaimed.

The Love Shack was our first home, where we would make two of our four babies. Seth wanted to follow his dream. That's why we moved there, so he could write music and travel fulltime, but then he settled out of the blue for law school. I was terrified. I had married a youth minister and musician. I had grown up down a dirt road. I knew nothing of men in suits except for those in church work. When I finally gave in to it, he held me across his lap in the recliner and I cried. I'm not sure what, but I remember that he promised me something.

I've always been able to move on quickly because I'm a worker. There's no use in wallowing long, I thought. I decided to have a party. I hadn't worn a tank top or listened to non-Christian music in over a year, and we didn't work for a church anymore. My bra straps were showing, and my back and shoulders were free. I found those blue jeans with a hole in the knee, and I mailed invitations for my own birthday. Our Love Shack had paneled walls and thirty-year-old shag carpet. I put candles in every room. I wanted fold-up chairs and tables and so many people we couldn't move. I wanted tough grapes dangling from a pretty tray, and I wanted to get lost in conversation. I wanted to think about theology and listen to Jimi Hendrix while I put on my makeup.

I never had been a good youth minister's wife, and he had decided to be a lawyer. He wanted to be right and have buying power, and I wanted to be a poet. I wanted to finish my degree in English. I wanted to sit in class and get lost with the lost. I wanted to commune with storytellers and picture painters. I wanted brave artist souls to love me like I'd never tried on church or looked like church or sounded like it. I invited whoever would come because the sick need company. Whatever disease the church had, we had caught it. Seth sat in the front room at my birthday party. I sat in the back.

We lived alongside one another, insatiable, but not for each other. We were together yet far apart in separate lives, bumping elbows as we brushed our teeth. Our skulls were cups that never got full.

Seth was leading worship for a huge college service, and we led Bible studies, because it was easy and we had our theology down pat. We just kept switching hard back and forth like a bicycle about to crash. From try-hard holy to secret-seeded desire, we flailed through our second year of marriage.

Our lives were almost full of promise. Grandma would make a huge Tupperware bowl of tuna fish salad and invite me over for lunch between my classes. She always added eggs, sweet relish, and Miracle Whip and put frozen wheat bread in the microwave. She placed the sandwiches on a beautiful plate with tiny pink and blue flowers around the gold rim. She cut the sandwiches into triangles and put a straw in my drink and a folded napkin to the side. She held my hand to pray. She was so proud of us.

We were the ones you called to do the right thing, the ones to help others through hard times. We were beautiful expectations, pedestaled leaders, perpetuating the very sickness that drove us to the Love Shack. We looked so healthy. Surely that healthy glow would reach to our hearts. Surely our righteousness would become legitimate when we did our next good thing.

I had learned well how to hide brokenness, how to send it buried down, work it away, but then I began to have a constant fever and unexplainable pain and swelling throughout my body. My skin broke and rashed and made doctors whisper *lupus* and *cancer*. I took rounds of steroids and had biopsies they called false negatives. I became the kind of tired that couldn't move and the sick no one could name. Everything felt suspicious. Was it in my head? Was it in what I was eating? Or was I self-inflicted with unforgiveness toward the church?

Desire when it is conceived gives birth to sin, and we desired to be better. We thought we were better than the church, but instead we were the church with an immunity disorder, I in bed at dusk and he in an office chair through the night.

I had been working on a paper about the poetry of Elizabeth Bishop when one early morning I sat at the computer to

begin working where I had left off the day before. I didn't know
Seth had been awake for hours after I had been at the screen. I
didn't expect the backspace to get me caught in the web he had
tangled in the night before. Back and back and back, I observed
in detail what it was that he craved, what had been feeding him
when he was hungry.

He was asleep under sheets yellow in the sun. I said his name,
standing beside the bed, and when he peeked up through morning eyes, I told him I had seen it all, back and back and back. I
had taken note of every face that wasn't mine. He reached his
arm up for my hand in the quick fear of one falling a long way
down, and I pulled away. "Don't touch me."

It wasn't long until law school began. As Seth disappeared
into books, I disappeared into my poetry and was accepted into
the master of fine arts program at the University of Arkansas
to study under world-class teachers.

We became half law, half poetry. Surely, if the words of the
Bible wouldn't sustain us, then these other words would. Surely,
we could make our own way, better than those in the church.
These aren't thoughts one knows she thinks, but surely we could
be better than the church.

Seth would come home, worn from passionate writing on
behalf of mistreated Muslims, and I lost care for him and his
work. I had no vision for his art: to dive and puzzle, review
the law. He was in the top ten of his class, and I would reach
my arms across the bed at 2:00 a.m. to find him finally home,

and then I would wake at 6:00 in an already empty bed. Once I told him I was an affair waiting to happen. I warned him, and he reached across the dinner table and cried. He said, "No. You're my best friend." And we really were. We really did love each other. When he was home, we would accidentally forget the hurt, and we would laugh so hard. We really always were best friends.

Love was burning low, but he played guitar and worked at the ashes. When he stopped his work long enough to be with me, he could always turn up a glow. There has always been a part of him that retrieves me, like one rushing with a blazing lantern into a sorcerer's den. The light in him was the light that shone over the surface of the oldest void. There was love, and that love always made me crave the light.

But becoming a student of poetry in a master of fine arts program can be like entering the hungry, immortalizing high school halls of vampires. We took in darkness, what hid in shadows. The worship of art is a powerful way to let go of religious self-awareness. Studying poetry was learning ancient rhythms for internal sonar. Poetry takes lines and breaks them. We wrote the dark side of prophecy. I took in a sick empathy for ones who write. Give me a poet knee-walking drunk. Give me a poet and his favorite nude art. Give me a poet and her window gaze. Give me her wicked sixth sense.

I was still playing church in the same way as those I had grown tired of while trying to sustain another part of my life by crafting beautiful words. I studied myself in a way that held me captive inside, honed in, looking for the next line, scrounging for nourishment from within. Oh, I was starving.

The hollow is made for a Holy Spirit that satisfies, and any other thing will only dry the bones and hush the prayer. I was trying to take hold of the freedom I thought I recognized among the writers, and I thought I recognized freedom because they welcomed me in.

I had always belonged in circles around bonfires in my comfortable, smoky spot in honest conversation. Writing workshops felt more soul-bare than Sunday school. A friend in the program once told me she thought people go to church to discuss how fabulous they are. My friends in that English department made me feel normal in my lack of fabulousness. They gave me a place to belong.

It was true, though, that I didn't belong there in the ways I wanted to. I didn't connect how I thought I might. I was younger than most in the program, and I was one of the only ones married. Intimacy was scarce, and no one knew what to do with vulnerability. Poetry is a private thing and had a way of splaying us all too bare. I wasn't ready for so much sadness.

Franz Wright came to teach for a semester and won his Pulitzer during his stay. I was in the first class he taught. We waited around an oval table. He came disheveled, his hair wild and the creases of his smile holding his glasses up. He read a few titles of poems we should know and decided to read one aloud to us. It felt like someone had walked in terrified and then had proceeded to get naked. His reading was slow. Our breaths sucked up inside us. We were holding. Not a sound. Then his voice cracked, and he stopped to catch the words in suspense, lest he cry in front of us all. That's when I knew I loved him, right away, someone broken.

It seemed that we were all a bit too broken, too close to the pain. I recognized familiar addictions in others there, too, but the thing I craved the most after one semester was joy and an honest-to-goodness, sober-as-hell, gut-busting laugh.

My poetry was made of backwoods fear, of the sweet oily chestnut, of the experienced gloves in Mama Lois's back closet, and of the charm and moan of guitars. My poetry was for desire, to satisfy the groans of my body and to write the aura of skin. It was for self-pleading, to understand myself as beautiful. But in the end, all I wanted was for someone to tell me a joke. I wanted someone to save me, to knock the breath out of me with laughter.

As Seth finished law school, I failed at right love, but we began to study the bodies beneath our own roof. We tried to make ourselves something new. We never stopped trying to make love. Seth came home early one afternoon. I had been eating and eating and eating. We sat to watch *The Simpsons*. He asked, "Are you pregnant?" I shook my head yes without looking away from the television, and we knew he was a boy because we'd dreamed of him. We knew we'd name him Isaac, and we knew Isaac means "laughter." No matter how much we craved the knee-slapping relief, the joy due to the moment, we were not yet to the punch line. We were still listening to the joke.

A Wolf Revision

I have a vision of us in our old age. Seth will pat my rear, take me around the world, and suffer my preaching. He will get me approximately twenty-two thousand glasses of water before bed and go looking for my lost phone at least half as many times. I will watch his butt disappear straight into his back. His hair will turn white, and mine will thin into flat ashen brown. He will look on as I droop and shimmy into jeans, and he will see the girl behind my eyes. He will sing to me. One of us will hear the other whisper to angels. There will be a sigh, a last strained grip of our hands, and then a slip behind the veil. Our bodies will cling even after one has gone. I have seen what we will become.

When I told him that we would be together until death, I didn't know that meant I should fling my love up like a guard rail around us, lay it down like a path, and build it up like walls and a roof. I didn't know we were shepherds with our love, to corral it into lush places. I didn't know our lives would become a canvas to be claimed by graffiti, that we would never stop painting and choosing to paint. There is a mantel in the mind's eye, the place that holds a heart's vision. No one told me to nail and spotlight a vision of our love above the mantel. No one told me that we will always be walking toward the place we set our eyes.

There were days I replaced the vision of our love with other pictures. I visited Ireland and sat with friends in a strumming pub where a man from Connemara asked me why I visited Galway. I answered poetry, and he whispered poets' names into my ear and talked of them quietly as music blared. He told me he could show me the island. He wanted to show me the sea. Even though I told him no and acted uninterested, a new idea had entered my mind just for fun, a new green canvas with craggy hills and raging water on which to fix my gaze when Seth called again and again to tell me he wouldn't be home.

I began to revise my future, as if the rewriting would make it better. Even when my eyes unhinged from the sea and reattached to Seth, I didn't know that with love I must constantly rehang the original art, repeatedly turn away from the version of myself that ran into the arms of another, and repeatedly deny the version of ourselves that didn't suffer. I saw myself in the past, in love, and I told her, "Revisions of love are perversions. You cannot revise the future for improvements. It is already beautiful—a garden planted, watered, pruned, and bearing fruit."

I had never felt more like a grown woman, a baby folded up inside like a fortune in a cookie. I said what I meant. I didn't have energy left for anything else. My necklines showed more than I had ever dreamed on my own body. I felt sexy and confident, more decided, wearing elastic waistbands earlier than I should. My lips were full, my eyes greener. I didn't know who I was, where my childlike was. I wanted to love that man who cooked me burned chicken when I craved it, and I did in the way that met on a bed and said excuse me at the bathroom mirror before heading out. But I said what I meant. He called to say he wouldn't be home from school until 2:00 a.m., and I said, "I don't care anymore. You don't even have to call me about it anymore," and I meant it.

The painting of the sea amused me enough, though I knew it wasn't real. The creative in me reached for the brush where I could find it.

Then in my office at the university, I saw something new, a new color palette. Pictures I had never seen splattered across my mind like thick beads of vibrant oil running down old visions. Secret thoughts of another man in my everyday life began to trickle over me so gradually that I switched imaginations without knowing it. I never thought of it as an affair, not the lying, not the exchange of poetry, not the longing, not the kiss. I didn't know what I meant anymore, so I didn't know how to say what it was.

Wolves can tend as shepherds, and I began to feel the wolf. I would have laid down the staff, the brush, switched roles, and pretended that wolfish thoughts were more lush to be able to leave my marriage, the pain, the thing that took so much energy to behold as precious. But I couldn't call the new thing an affair because it was never actually good, never the same beautiful scene I had once known with Seth.

It was a short, powerful season, and then I turned hard, chiseling desperate against the revisions, aching between bone-deep guilt and a beggar's prayer.

Isaac began to stretch inside me, tapping gently at first, then rolling sharp elbows in long lines beneath the tearing muscles. I was stretching at my core. Beneath my rib cage, I burned, and every ache felt like a truth, so I sang to the stretching. God has used a child's body as his own more than we think. I grabbed Seth's hand and held it to the movement.

This is when I saw the vision, what we will become, these very hands holding his when the last sigh becomes our parting. This is when I began the weak clinging.

Look above the mantel now. Look at the ultrasound. There's a new face drawn there. He is law and poetry spliced into one beating heart.

Thirsty

Three days after my due date, I sat on the edge of my bed and felt the mattress bend beneath my massive rear end, and I moaned in a fully surrendered belief that this monster baby would grow and live inside me forever. I cried and whimpered for Seth to bring more water and decided on a lifetime of beached-whale feelings.

Then at 3:00 a.m. the waters broke. Time slowed, and slight contractions had me wading ankle-deep. My head was well above water, and I was able to see our lives for what they were. We were two about to be three. I swayed through the hospital feeling the weight of it. We had been married for five years. We had walked up this long shore, and there we were walking in, as for a baptism.

A burn pulled low. I held on to Seth and made sure the nurses knew I wouldn't need help. Natural childbirth was the plan, and it was something we had decided to do, just us, though we weren't brave enough for a home birth.

I agreed they could hear the baby's heart for a bit, so they put a band around me, and we could hear him like a knock on a microphone. The screen showed I was contracting, which is exactly when I began to feel it. They told me to let them know if I needed anything at all, and I couldn't explain the thirst.

I pushed the nurse's button on the bed, and after a few moments, I heard her voice from somewhere. I didn't know where. She kept saying, "May I help you?" and I couldn't tell how to respond. My brain had been eking for ten slow months, which has to explain why I suddenly thought, *Oh, she's in the microphone on my tummy.* So I lifted the neck of my gown and peeked down to all the round places and said, "Uh, am I allowed to have some water?"

"Only ice chips, ma'am." I looked at Seth and shrugged "oh well." And then he asked me, "What were you just doing? Who do you think you were talking to down there?" And that's when it hit me. Oh. There are speakers on the bed.

We laughed hard, so hard that I slobbered and wiped tears from my cheeks. Seth kept talking down his shirt, and I would respond down my gown. We laughed like kids in a garden, like people who loved good, like we were best friends, and I look back on it like it was the spring of our marriage, like the side splitting was the sky breaking open with rain.

Waves of laughter peeled out, and it wasn't long before something more animal than laughter began. My back spread out flat and labor deepened. Ten-second breaks between contractions weren't long enough to catch a gasp. A baby likes to twist down and into the world like a corkscrew unwinding. Oh, but this one just wanted to burrow through slow and straight. He wanted to come out looking at the sky. For seventeen hours I thought my back would break. The monitor flatlined up top.

Seth kept with me. He would touch the strain in my face, and I would relax it. I gave in. He loved me. He studied me, every single tension of my body. Before I left my mind completely, I was watching us become something, laboring, giving in. The pain swell turned me on my hands and knees like a beast with my nakedness exposed. Waves were crashing, but there was Seth holding float. I remembered every word to "I Surrender All," and it moved me forward, deeper. I made up new words.

My girlfriend Brooke put her fists into me and put her feet into the wall to hold for strength. A nurse came in and made me hold one end of a towel. She yelled and woke into my mind and said, "Push!" Another nurse and Brooke held my knees, but Seth kept my eyes. He didn't break contact. We were forehead to forehead. My back moaned, and then a baby ripped out. There we had finally done it. We had made ourselves Love.

We had made ourselves humble, weak, and clinging. We had made ourselves a baby, and I was exhausted. Seth kept water by my hospital bed and held Isaac. When my body brought forth life, my secret pushed to the front, too, a tinged sort of beauty: *I am so loved by my husband, but I have desired another man.*

I held that precious baby and thought, *Doesn't love hate a secret?*

We brought Isaac home, tightly burritoed and jammed with blankets and buckles into a car seat, and we introduced him to our curious dog before I waddled to the bed, where family joined us. For days friends dropped off food, and Seth entertained them. My milk came, and Isaac had no trouble. I would stare and stare at him. I would undo his blanket and look him all over. I studied his fingernails and the way his legs bent and the gray of his wide-open eyes. His eyes were nebulas to me, like seeing into galaxies.

Our first night home, I leaned over Isaac's blank gaze and told him every single thing I could think about Jesus, like there were worlds inside him that might need to hear. I felt silly but did it anyway. I spoke to him until I drifted to sleep, only to gasp awake every few minutes with my hand on his chest to see if he was still breathing, as if my paying attention was what kept him alive.

I wound up so tightly in the opposite direction of rest. I tightened up into a willed machine, clenched at my baby and my secrets. Only in exhaustion would I bow low in prayer, always hiding parts away because I couldn't let them go. I was always aware that this was my second baby and that I could have torn this family apart with an affair.

Instead, we were learning to love. Seth kept his hand on my back, where I needed it in labor. He stayed present. Neither of us wanted to miss a thing and treated Isaac as if he had been the first baby child to enter the world. When we left the house, we would look around dumbfounded at folks. Didn't they know Isaac was born? I saw Seth in his handsome face. We took pictures of every drooling twitch of his lips. We fed him baby food that made him gag, and then I decided to make my own baby food, organic, of course. I spent money and hours cooking, and grinding, and pureeing, and all the while, Isaac had crawled to the doggy bowl and was eating dog food. Seth and I laughed all the time, constantly taking note, we in baby journalism.

Once in a while, a stage hits that feels beautiful and slow. Those first months as a mother, our marriage floated as on glass, and we were philosophers. We would sit outside after Isaac went to sleep, and we would listen to music. We had time to imagine that one day Isaac would walk down an aisle. It would be graduation or marriage. He wouldn't be thinking about his mama and her crazy love, or the books we read together, or the attacks of the tickle monster, but I would. We would remember our baby. Seth would squeeze my hand. We discussed how our memories of Isaac were for us, for me and the one who bought my diamond after only one month, the one who became my kin and worked at my glowing ashes. In the memory making, we weren't bonding only with the child.

We were enmeshing and drinking it in together. We were extending ourselves, as in lovemaking, into the other's heart. We were healing, strengthening, growing. I knew even then that one day I would think of that tiny hot body and his miniature hand in my shiny hair, how I poured out like a fountain, how thirsty I was, and I would remember how Seth never failed to bring me water.

Four months into parenting, one evening I bounced that teething baby on my jutted hip. I opened the curtains, the day bending navy, and I waited for the rock-crackle of the driveway, for the car lights, for Seth to walk in, and for the baby to lean into stronger arms. He came home from his law firm with no break from work except a song on the drive, and I handed Isaac over, cracked my back, then hid in the laundry room in an unartistic collapse at my desk like a bag of sand pouring. We were in a stage of pouring. We were both then in constant thirst, water glasses lining our little house, all to be hand-washed. We were learning small capacity, how to stack at the sink, how to fold baby clothes into drawers with notebooks.

We learned the mother-shaped body, the lawyer-tired, the timing, how it holds together by prayer, by small touch, by little acts—a dropper of Tylenol in the night. And then, somehow, again, two pink lines rose on a pregnancy test. They would be fourteen months apart, and we dazed through two months of shocked happy faces. The Little Parents Who Could: *I think I can I think I can I think I can*. In the bewildering excitement, the work to keep nursing, always drinking, ever being filled, I began to bleed.

I doubled on the floor over stacked pillows while Isaac rolled and laughed, the dog strangely aware of his charge, and I poured out again. Back to back, my third and my fourth babies went this way, straight to God. As helplessly grieved as we've ever been in the releasing, we learned in it somehow a delight. I had hoped that I would take rest in God during another heartbreak, but only when the breaking happens can anybody really know. There were moments it seemed that Jesus had literally walked in our door to sit with us on the couch. We were hurt, but we understood our control in the matter, and we understood that God was there, bending low to the broken, and that his being with us was something we wouldn't change. Our hearts stretched out like wineskin, with the capacity for two more without ever having them fill our arms. Oh, how we held each other, and we didn't talk much about it—how we spilled out like cracked cups, how even in death we brimmed with something that felt like life.

We moved from the Love Shack to the first neighborhood of my entire country life, with a park and dogs and kids who ding-dong ditch. It was a grand house in my scheme of things—three bedrooms total and a living room with a tall, well-lit ceiling. I decorated. My mama made my curtains, and they were beautiful. I put everything in a place exactly how grown-ups are supposed to. Another baby was on his way, our Jude, to be born twenty-one months after Isaac. I knew somehow that he would be an artist, how he pushed me from within and then slid his leg or arm the diameter round, feeling his space, filling his space.

Seth planted seeds in a flower bed, babies of his own, his first working at dirt. He thought of them in the night and had sprinklers scheduled to water them in perfect intervals.

I, too, thought in the night how lovely it would be for something to mind my clock. I needed the baby out. By my eighth month, the doctors had put me on bed rest, and Seth was working and working the dirt, hot peppers huge in the backyard.

When no one was watching, I bought castor oil, and I drank it followed by Coke—nastiest thing I've ever done. Then I waited for the burn again and the consistent back strain. I breathed steadily and rocked on my feet. I labored, and Seth worked gently along.

Then the drums started. It was dark out. And the drums started. And the drums kept drumming, inconsistent, bad drumming in a garage with teenagers who grew loud and showed tiny cracks up from their jeans. In an oiled stupor, I rose. I leaned through the front door into summer night, barefooted and pregnant, and I stomped, having just had a contraction. I had just enough time to make it to their yard. I paused to breathe, and then I walked in their grass, introduced myself as a neighbor in labor at night, and I told them to hush, and their eyes were wide moons, and they said, "Yes, ma'am." And the drumming stopped, and so did my contractions. I was so mad.

Sometimes the body misleads, all this work we have to do when the garden isn't made for us anymore. It's a curse to feel the need to step in, bound by time and pain. God is invisible, so we induce. He is invisible, but we are in him, even when we try to lead.

At the hospital again, I labored to six centimeters, and then our round baby, a fast and passionate one, was at my breast within ten minutes. I covered the bed in so much blood. Seth smothered in the idea of losing. I was pale white, holding Jude, and Seth cornered himself in the room all blank, and it hit me, again, how he loved me; how I loved what he planted; how I loved my Jude; how he moved in bulk, studying faces; how gently he undid all our swaddling—full bloom from the beginning.

⚜

I spent my days skin on skin, our two little boys clinging. One attention hound took his hands and held my face to speak to my eyes from an inch away so I would see into his imagination. Isaac was two and talked like a ten-year-old about alligators and outer space. The other one nursed like an obsessive-compulsive vacuum cleaner. I hardly kept up. Jude was only four months old and what we called a hoss. He would drink and pet my collarbone and sing through every gulp. He had teeth, beautiful boy, wide brown eyes, but my milk turned shy because I couldn't drink enough, and I feared the latch. I thought, *What will be left of me after this?*

Seth sang them love ballads from the early eighties. He propped them on the edge of our bed and played like he had a mullet and tight pants. No one played air guitar like that man. We loved to laugh more than ever, and my house was clean when we went to bed at night. I felt officially good at my phase of life, but the truth behind the grind was that I was touch exhausted. I was wearing and carrying and nursing. My lap was never free.

Seth and I slept beneath the same blanket, our pillows together, a prayer tossed between us. We were on repeat. Morning always came and took him to the wolves, and I missed him always, even when we were in the same room.

The days blurred into a season. They blurred so that we didn't see the melding, the continuation of two becoming one. We were together, but to touch, to actually find an intimate place that didn't feel used up, it took prayer. So I prayed daily for desire and the passion that caused us to become engaged after only two months. All day I thought about him. I washed his clothes. I watched his boys turn into little versions of him. And one night, after a bad movie and a good bottle of wine, the desire for desire finally won.

Two weeks later, I woke early, before anyone else. In the quiet, morning light bursting white on our walls, two pink lines surfaced again, and then a flood of tears and unexpected gratitude. *How? Can I handle three babies in three years?* I held it secret in a long shower, and I cried, and I heard God speak, like I was a canyon and he was an echoing whisper. He said he would care for us, and I didn't have any other choice but to believe him.

Holding the hand of a toddler and carrying a baby on the side of my ginormous belly was the most physically exhausting thing I have ever done. At the time I was just doing what I had to do, but now I look back on it and I see how incredible it was. It's no secret. An honest woman who can keep a baby and a toddler alive while making another human inside her body knows deep down the truth of strength in weakness. Never is there a stronger kind of weak. I would get so tired at the grocery store that I would sit down in the aisle and tell people to just walk around me. Once I broke in line at the deli and told everybody I had to get my turkey before my baby came out on the linoleum. When I walked into a room, crowds would part down the middle. Once I sat in a chair at church, and it nearly parted down the middle too. I became a powerful and large woman, and all the while I was teaching Isaac Bible verses. I was the southern, souped-up cliché version of the Proverbs 31 woman back then and as miserable as I could possibly be.

During that time, as my body expanded, my heart would skip beats or add an extra twenty. From time to time, I felt a wave of intense anxiety and would nearly faint, and a heart monitor couldn't catch any of the glitches. Sometimes it was as if my heart couldn't keep up with all it contained, and other times it would throw itself into overdrive to push me through.

When labor began with our third son, Ian, we went to the hospital as usual. It was my shortest, most confident labor. It was slowed, stalled, then superfast just as with Jude, but then at the end, as the waves started crashing down, every grip I had seemed to loosen. The hospital had lassoed the sunshine in through those lamps, and I was spotlighted from every direction, not a shadow in the room. But even then, the lights began to dim. In my southern drawl, I told the nurses, "My heart's running away with me," and they looked at me with a smile as if to say "Aw, that's so sweet you're excited." But what I was saying was that my heart was actually and in fact running so fast that I felt I was leaving my body. I couldn't get my words to connect with any of our brains.

It wasn't long before the nurses were yelling, "Don't push!" But I had no control and had relaxed into a heart rate of 230 beats per minute. Unbeknownst to us all, the monitor had been recording my heart instead of the baby's, and it had been flipping at that pace for over thirty minutes. My body delivered Ian without my mind involved. I was a limp, surrendered girl slipping down a quiet tunnel. My memory plays it in slow motion. They yell, "Stat," and then an intercom calls. Nurses are running in every direction, jabbing my IV, taking my baby to the warming table. The doctor yells. All the brows furrow. Seth asks, "Is she okay? Is she okay? Is she okay?" until all sounds mute, and I don't know if I'll hold my baby before my heart explodes. Tears and high-pitched awes pour rightly over Ian. The camera snaps.

They pumped me with beta-blockers and had no idea what had happened, other than that adrenaline can apparently flip my switch hard. I had naturally overdosed myself. My usual heart rate is a slow thing. My usual blood pressure hardly indicates that I'm alive at all. So when I was on beta-blockers, I floated far away, barely attached to my body. I went from having blood so fast that it was whooshing straight through to blood so slow that I was floating above the room. I saw Seth darting his eyes between fear and joy. I saw him stay with me like a hitching post. He called toward Ian with the sweetest voice while still holding my hand. Finger to my wrist, he counted the ways of my heart.

Secret
Hiding Place

In the field, across the fence and halfway to the old strawberry patch, there was a circle of small, branchy trees that leaned inward, like a round of dancing women holding hands. In the summer, they wore green dresses and had honeysuckle hair. In the winter, you could see the strong bones and a weave of vines like gray ribbons.

I hunted once with Daddy near there. We crouched in the tree line and shot at a flutter of doves. The dog ran out and we followed. We walked by the circle, and I didn't even tell him what it was: my hiding place. It's where I ran when the world felt mad. I had a secret place whose arms tangled round me. I sat in the middle and had a window to the sky.

I wonder how many hiding places I've had since then, what friends, foods, and journals. Mazzy Star, Pearl Jam, and Smashing

Pumpkins on my mixed tapes hid me. There was a parking spot behind a tiny church off Simpson Point Road that hid me. I've hidden in poetry, drugs, theology, music, and men.

The hiding place is always the secret.

With every labor, I remember the direction of my bed and the height of the sun. With Ian, the day was edging in burnt orange to my right as a steadier heartbeat brought my mind back to my body. I needed my mind to be able to bond and teach him to drink while my body did the work of clenching back into shape from within. The room was chaos and the pain severe, but Ian was easy to hold close. Our bond was strong. Seth leaned in, and we wondered if he was human at all. He had the face of an angel, an extra light in him. From the day he learned to connect eyes, he looked at us like we were everything good, like he knew a beautiful secret between God and the rest of us. When he learned to talk, he told us that he came from inside God. The first time I held him, I knew that much.

He was a gift of joy and something otherworldly, and thank goodness for that, because recovery took months. Not only had I brought home a baby, but I had also picked up way too many cardiology appointments along with bronchitis and stitches, which is not a good combination. I had birthed three babies in three years: Ian (fresh out); Jude (thirteen months old and eating crayons); and Isaac, my jabber-baby (three years old the day we came home from the hospital).

It may be necessary to pause here. Let it soak in. Three babies in three years doesn't set any records, but it sure does add a unique bunch of transforming characters to my narrative in a very short period of time. We could feel ourselves being changed by the minute, and change was exactly what we wanted. We always said we wanted to be different, to live different, kind, world-changing lives, but when it came down to it, we had been everything but different with our big house and fine job and cute dog. We kept our machine oiled and our lives beautiful, but to add three children in three years was to bring a kind of messy you can't pretend around.

We had decided months before that, soon after Ian's birth, Seth would visit our friends in Mozambique, and even before he left, I felt a shift coming. The day I dropped him off at the airport to send him to Africa while I cared for three children, my focus took a hard turn inward. Ian became extremely sick that day with RSV, and a few days later, he stopped breathing in my arms, turned blue, then grunted and re-pinked. I stayed awake alone well beyond what one does with a newborn to feel the rise and fall of his chest, and in all the unrest, awake all night, my mind returned again and again to my secret. I hid myself at night in the guilt of that affair I had with someone I didn't love. The secret was filling me, and all I desired was freedom from it.

When Seth returned from Africa, he cried and spilled the most beautiful, despairing, and contradictory set of details. I loved him and never wanted to see him hurt. Our ride home was covered in fear, what was happening within Seth, within me, how Ian wasn't the only one suffocating.

Weeks later, Ian could breathe without my watch, Seth would wake at 4:00 a.m. to find his breath in prayer, and I hoped heart surgery would fix my ache. I had continued to experience chest pain, arrhythmias, and floods of anxiety.

The cardiologist scheduled exploratory surgery where a tiny scope took a drive inside my heart. During surgery, they dosed me with adrenaline, and I woke from the anesthesia. I remember the doctor's surprise right there in the middle of it as he said, "Oh!" while my heart banged so hard that my body bounced. He told me afterward that I am sensitive to adrenaline, and I have too much electricity firing in my heart, which made plenty of sense to me.

I needed an ablation, and I'm not a doctor, so this is how I understood it: the doc enters the heart with a zapper on a long cord, makes my heart fire wildly, and then deadens the heart in the places that told my heart to rev. The actual surgery took five hours, and when it was over, the doctor said it was *mostly* successful. He was able to turn the electricity down, but he wasn't able to deaden it all the way without putting in a pacemaker. The chances of me having another episode were slim but still possible.

My life was more beautiful than ever, but inside my head, fear, anxiety, and depression overwhelmed me. I started to drown, whirlpooling deeper into my own mind. Outside of me was a shove from bottle to sink to laundry to bed; garage to grocery to church; spoon to mouth; mascara to eye. It was tick of clock and refrigerator hum and children playing, and in the mind-whirl was fear of death, little inhales of water, a choking on images, the sound of roosters crowing.

Anxiety is like dying of thirst and not knowing how to drink the water you swim in. Anxiety can be like thoughts on a circuit or being caught in a riptide. It's like living a hair away from electric shock and a breath away from inhaling the river.

After surgery, I visited the doctor again and again because of chest pain, and every time he told me the pain wasn't coming from my heart. I gasped awake every night with my heart racing. I took Seth's hands and begged that he pray away the panic that had interrupted deep sleep.

I pretended wine would help. I imagined shopping on the internet would protect my thoughts. I acted like a clean house would put my heart in order or that more sex would erase the sin. But then the wine ran out. The milk spilled. The package arrived at the door, and it all spun me deeper and faster into the whirling. I was drowning in the sameness of our culture, and my head was spinning so hard that I found myself begging like one who had never known herself to be loved.

If I give you more and buy less, will you love me then?

If I lead another Bible study, will you make me stable?

If I teach them more Bible verses, will they be easier to handle?

There was no rest. There never is for the one who desires to fit but doesn't believe she is loved.

My chest never stopped hurting, as if the anesthesia from surgery had just worn off, like all the feeling was trying to come back at once, as if they had decided to leave the scope inside my rib cage. There was something inside thrashing around. There was something that wanted out.

I thought anxiety had to bow to my Christian bidding. All the names of Jesus I knew weren't moving the shadow. There was no obedient "get thee behind me." I looked the pain and the fear straight in the eyes and told it all to go to hell, but it wouldn't budge.

One night fear so jolted my sleep that I woke foot-stomping angry. I was so mad that my prayer was more like a yell. I tore into the throne room, knowing exactly who was there. "I see you there, God, on your throne, and I know you can change this. Why aren't you healing me?"

Then he threw me from there, from my open-eyed prayer, into a deep, rare sleep. I stepped into a dreamworld where my living room was crisp clean, so I went to the backyard to clean the toys from there. There were play mats and bouncy seats and other big toys, and as I tried to pick up each one, from underneath a giant snake uncoiled. Snakes were under everything.

I woke terrified again with an excruciating pain in my chest. "What is it, God? Snakes are so cliché. Please don't make me tell Seth. Please. Please, don't make me tell him." Then quickly away to sleep, I dreamt again. My living room was perfectly clean, so I went to the back door to straighten the toys there. As I opened the door, snakes poured into my house. Waist high, they hissed, and I couldn't easily shut the door. They slithered in and hid beneath the toys in baskets.

I woke again, with the kind of calm heart that happens after a trauma. "Okay. I'll tell him, but you'll have to help me."

Then to make sure I understood it, I dreamt again, a third dream. Snakes writhed on every toy in the house. They had taken over.

When I woke, it was day but still dark, and Seth was already awake and sitting in the lamplight in the living room. I walked in unrested and noticed his distressed face. "What's wrong?" I said. He had had dreams that night, too, so he outright asked me, "I hate to do this, but I need to know if there's something you need to tell me."

I sat down next to him in shock. I was on the end of the couch. He was in the chair. Until that very moment, I had feared the pain of hurting him with the truth more than I had feared God or my sin patterns passing to my children. I said, "Yes. I have to tell you that I kissed him."

The despair was palpable. He cried with an ache that outdid any chest pain I had experienced. *Grief* doesn't seem word enough. An immediate, deep awareness filled our house, and the sun rose up. I had had an affair four years before I confessed it, so nothing new had happened except our sudden shared knowledge of how broken we were, and it was more than a knowing of the mind. We could feel it. It was down to the bone emotion. It was right out in the air how broken. I was splayed wide open, exposed, in a name of Jesus I hadn't remembered in a long time. He is my Hiding Place. In the light of that morning, there wasn't a shadow left for hiding. It's called mercy when the rays beat down and we're forced out of the shadows. I had no secret hiding place left that wasn't in my Jesus, that wasn't in his mercy.

Add one tiny bit of yeast to a lump of dough, and it will leaven the entire thing. This is the way of a lie. Throw a lie into a relationship, and the entire thing will be scrutinized as a lie.

Why wouldn't it be? At first, even the truth didn't feel like the truth to Seth, but it did to me. All the grief I had ever experienced before that moment felt like a slap on the wrist compared to watching his agony. My confession unraveled that man, and he questioned my every thought, every promise I had ever made.

I had nowhere to go to run from that kind of pain. The next day in the shower, I moaned. I had no control of my despair. Mascara ran down to my thighs.

I didn't know what to do with myself. I turned the water off, stepped out, and pulled the towel down to my face. My body dripped all over. His were the arms of my comfort, and he walked in to me. I wanted him to embrace me, but instead he approached me and grabbed me by my shoulders, and I was clean and dripping down. He said, "Listen." Then his words poured like a cold shock.

"Please forgive me," he said. "Please forgive me for leaving you during law school." He said "forgive me" for other things too. I had been completely unaware that I hadn't forgiven. My sin had so overshadowed his that I never realized how I harbored unforgiveness, which has a way of skewing perspective. Along with guilt, unforgiveness had been my haven of unrest. Unforgiveness had been my hiding place.

I gave him his forgiveness, and he gave me mine. I fit in his arms like a conquered puzzle.

The next day he bought me an emerald, small, square, and surrounded by tiny diamonds. He spent all the money we had to buy it, to hang a vision of what we had become around my neck. He wanted to start it all from scratch, without a hint of leavening.

I wanted him, and we loved like we had put on brand-new skin. We thought to ourselves, *Let us never grow old; let us hear the other breathe; let me call your depravity my own; let us call this unity the two becoming small, new, kindled, one.*

He said he didn't want big anymore, enough with this big house. He said enough with wanting to go big and made promises we'd be big enough to do all the big things it takes to be just good enough. From then on, we decided together: we are small. We are a precious thing. We know so little. We were new.

Doula

Through my entire childhood, I never once imagined growing up to be a mom. I only ever assumed that I would be a mamaw, like the mamaw I loved so much. I was nearly grown before I figured out that in order to be a mamaw, I would need to actually birth my own kids first, and I didn't desire to have children until maybe one month before I got pregnant. It was always something I figured would happen whether or not desire had anything to do with it, but if I did ever imagine it, I imagined two little girls. One would be like me and the other would be like my sister, who has been my lifelong, deepest friend, like someone who nearly shares a brain with me. I imagined that I would live in the country and have a tiny pool in the yard, where june bugs like to swim, and my daughters would play there like mermaids. I slowly came to imagine that a fulfilled life would be to see my own children experience the most gorgeous parts of my childhood. My sister is one of the most beautiful parts of my life. And if I had two girls, wouldn't Mamaw be so proud of me then? She would know then that I would be cared for, how her own daughter had cared for her.

Seth and I had been married for only a year when Mamaw's cancer took over, and I nearly left the transmission of a borrowed car with a stick shift on the side of Interstate 40 to get to her. She was in pain in Tennessee, and so I braved my own inability to drive a stick by hopping in the first car offered to me and having to start and restart that engine about five hundred times in the slow, stopping traffic of road construction clear through the middle of Arkansas. When I arrived at her bedside, I was thoroughly mortified. I was exhausted and couldn't believe I had made it.

Her face was still tinted with a smile, but she suffered worse than should be possible. I gulped hard and faced it in a hurry. Then something rose up in me that I didn't know was there. I was a doula. I was helping her be born into a new body. I was there to hope her through. My daddy's sister, Aunt Josie, had kept by her side for many months, but this was the stage that took round-the-clock care, so I joined her and watched a daughter work tirelessly out of a reservoir so full of love that she could have gone on that way for years. I didn't know anybody could stay awake for days like that just to hold someone's hand. Some things teach you what you're made of. My mamaw taught me until the very end.

Two other grandparents would go this way, and I saw the veil grow thin both times. When Seth's grandparents grew ill, I watched my mother-in-law press pause on her life. She sang to Grandmom. She rubbed her skin with beautiful lotion and steered her heart toward gratitude. They made lists together. She would lean near Grandmom's winced face and say, "What are your ABCs of thanksgiving?" Grandmom would respond in the voice of one in labor: "God is awesome. His world is beautiful. In heaven, I'll be with C. S. Lewis."

Then with Granddad, I watched her crawl in his bed like his baby child. She called him Daddy, and he called her Princess. She fed him by spoon and straw and tiny doses of morphine, and I assisted her both times. We worked together day and night. I watched another daughter give out of that reservoir, and seeing such love taught me how capable I was to suffer alongside.

My best friend chose natural childbirth. She was the first of us to birth a baby, her baby girl, and I was by her side (as I would be for all three of her births and she would be for all four of mine). When I put my hands on her back, while her husband kept her afloat, I could feel in my spirit and in the energy between our bodies exactly how hard to press and exactly where to press. This is kooky talk, but I look on it now and recognize the winds of the Holy Spirit speaking to me. I knew during those thin places of suffering that God was very near, that the ground was barefoot holy, and that his voice was clear to my heart. He sustained me mentally, spiritually, and physically in a shocking way, as I served in suffering.

Though it was the Spirit of God who made those experiences precious to me, it was seeing the love between a daughter and a parent that gave me a want, a desire so deep that I quickly pursued the adoption of our daughter after Ian was born. In fact, adoption had been an agreement that Seth and I had made before we were married. We said we would adopt "the least of these," meaning we would adopt one from among those least likely to be adopted. When we were first married, we knew no one who had adopted. It was an out-of-the-ordinary desire at the time, and it felt godly.

⁂

When we moved to the Rock House, we inherited a decade of vines wrapped into endless pretzels and slung up through the trees like knots of Tarzan swings. The boys could peel them back like a curtain and make secret hideout tunnels through the woods. We were covered in chiggers and mosquitoes, but it was worth it to feel close to the country again. A beautiful heron with green wings tiptoed through the pond until one by one the fish were gone. The waters rippled with tadpoles, and in the evening, toads belched in rhythm while tree frogs sang in between.

My house and my heart were full of boys and hero action figures and light sabers. They were catching things on fire and climbing heart-attack high at early ages. My laundry room floor was a mess of rocks, dirt, pine straw, and random, rusty metalwork from farm days past. All the jeans had grass-stained knees. The driveway would collect good-sized puddles, and they would play in the mud beneath the magnolia tree.

We grew squash, peppers, tomatoes, and every herb. Our lives didn't depend on it, but we were close enough to the dirt that we prayed for rain. I wore my little emerald necklace. We were small, and anything that helped us live that way felt like a healing. It felt like home.

Home is all we were ever really looking for.

As soon as Grandma said she wanted to move closer to her kids, we knew that moving into her old house was the exact downsize we needed. We assumed our big house would sell, so we moved, but then the real estate market crashed, and we were stuck with two mortgage payments. Practically, this helped a great deal with the desire to be small. We had no choice but to cut back, and we felt more desperate than ever to follow the small ways of Jesus. We felt our well-being depended on it.

As we renovated and decorated the house, I made a room for my daughter. Twenty-five miles up the road from us was a small community of friends who were in the adoption process as well. We were all adopting from Ethiopia, so they scooped us up and showed me how to create a three-inch, ringed binder with enough paperwork to make a brain explode.

During these days, we drove to them every Saturday morning and ate cinnamon rolls the size of our heads, and we laughed so hard every time. Seth had dance-offs with the kids, and we talked about any ole thing, paint-shallow and Bible-deep. We never set out to create community, but the common bond of adoption pulled us all together, and we were tight.

Most of the women were older than I, and they were beautiful and simultaneously messy. They would get together and invite me up for lunch and ask me questions. They would confess their own struggles about their marriages and parenting. They helped me keep my kids in line. This community was something new to me, like church without any sort of production, and it was all a part of being small, my being the one in the room with the least amount of wisdom.

There was something about being small that seemed to allow for us to do great big things for the kingdom of God. We were big on adoption, and we were big on community. This circle of friends could outwork a team of mules. We figured that living small meant making room for doing great big God things. We were known as the do-good people.

I was falling more and more in love with Ethiopia and her daughters by the day as we waited through the adoption process. We were listening to Ethiopian music and looking up videos and articles to glean anything we could from the culture.

One afternoon I was sitting in my kitchen, and Seth called to tell me he had emailed me a link, an exposé about Ethiopian adoption fraud, how on occasion mothers were not being told the truth about adoption. Perhaps they were told that their children were being taken to the West as exchange students or that they would return with great American wealth to rescue the family from poverty. Sometimes the mothers were bribed, while other times the children were sold by a relative. Then we moved on to videos in which mothers were saying good-bye to their children, and they were weeping and inconsolable. Many obviously didn't want to let their babies go but felt that they must.

I immediately told Seth that the videos were ridiculous and could not represent the majority of the stories. Surely most mothers were not being told any lies and were the bravest women to give up their babies. The only answer was to serve the least of these through adoption, so we needed to continue to pray that God would send us the remaining $20,000 it would take to finish the process. In my desire for a daughter and in my desire to change the world, I refused to listen to Seth or the Spirit.

Then he asked me to call our agency to see what they had to say about the stories we were hearing. How could we know that adoption fraud wasn't happening in Ethiopia through the orphanages where our potential daughter would live? I was furious that he had asked me to do it. I wanted nothing more than I wanted my daughter, but I called, and the worker assigned to us could not answer my questions. She said, "If God has told you to adopt, then don't question him." Later, Seth called someone with a little more knowledge about the Ethiopia side of things, and they smoothed over the questions, assured him that we were doing the work of the gospel. After all, hadn't Christ adopted us into his family at any cost?

I had no interest in knowing anything about adoption ethics. I had no interest in questioning my own desires to have a daughter. Why did I want a daughter from Ethiopia? Why not another son? Why not a child with special needs? I didn't want to know my answers, and I wanted to trust the adoption agency and every single person who stood with their hands outstretched, each who wanted a piece of the $20,000 standing between me and my daughter.

Pink dresses were hanging in my closet. I bought her little leather shoes with ladybugs on them, and I had her name monogrammed on an Easter basket liner: Abrihet, Abri for short. It means "she brings light" or "she shines." When I thought of her, my heart lit up. It was as innocent and natural as I had ever felt to want her.

The agency's inability to answer our questions, and their obvious discomfort, was shining its own light. Somewhere, my desires began to feel dark, but I was willing to deny it. Seth had a stronger persuasion, so it was clear that the timing was not right for us to continue with our adoption. Not only had our agency been exposed by their inability to answer our questions, but I also saw motives inside myself that were not considerate. I saw myself willing to ignore the possible injuries caused by my desire.

Our hearts were at a crossroad. As far as we could see, both ways turned toward heartache. There was no way around the pain of it. Even if the child was a double orphan, she would lose her extended family members. I didn't know of anyone who considered how to keep these families together. It was all broken.

I have heard again and again comparisons between birth and adoption, all the ways that adopting a child is like carrying one on the inside. I had never considered being pregnant with such desire, such longing to finally be home with our whole family, then to find myself laboring for something that wasn't going to come to pass.

When I began to feel the pain of it, of my not bringing home a daughter, I became aware of the cries of other mothers, their not being able to keep their children. I had an urge to push: prayer after prayer that the mother of Abrihet would become capable of caring for her own. I desired for daughters to come forth and become mothers with their own Amharic cries.

When we canceled our adoption, I labored, and then I wept in bed for months. I had held Abrihet in my heart, and I still do today. I just carry her, the light that she shined, in a different way.

Shortly after canceling, we learned of an organization called Kidmia that reunites children with families who've struggled to keep their little ones in the home, and we learned that Kidmia initiates in-country adoptions. In addition, Ethiopians were beginning to adopt Ethiopians for as little as $300. Our simple questions left us in shock for many months. Where do tens of thousands of dollars go between the United States and Ethiopia? This was happening worldwide. We could fund one hundred Ethiopian adoptions for the cost of our one adoption.

Our questions isolated us from community; whether self-imposed or not, we knew that our decision felt like a judgment. We wanted nothing more than to carry on how we had been. When they brought their babies home, I was so glad. The fruit of their own labors, the most beautiful kids in the world, live right here in Arkansas, and they are our joy. I wouldn't have it another way, but it wasn't meant to be for us.

We, in our Rock House with our beautiful boys, hit a heartbroken and lonely low, and that was not the kind of small we were looking for. We weren't looking for more heartache. We wanted a family that felt whole, a family that fit into a broad scheme of healing, on a local and a global scale. We had been surrounded by doulas, a community cheering us on in our labor of adoption, and suddenly, desire gave way to a stillbirth.

We had the ache of Africa inside us from Mozambique to Ethiopia. We had the ache of having known a community of friends who needed to stay on the adoption path, while we had to step to the side. We began the adoption process in obedience but had never experienced taking one path with an expected end to find that the intention of that path was to take us into the wilderness.

All along, we had three boys, and we wanted to be home with them. Over and over again, the wilderness was our home. We were burdened for justice in a broken system, desirous of community, and begging for healing in our own home. Low down, we wanted to thrive, and we didn't know the tiniest thing about how to live it. If anything was small, it was our hope.

I hadn't really connected with Lindsey in several years, but we were longtime, trusted friends. When she called me from Southeast Asia, she had no idea what was going on in my life, and I was just as clueless about hers. She was calling to tell me they were moving home, and they were about as broken and lonely and empty as they could be. I cried. Some of the tears were that I hated to hear her in pain, and some of the tears were my gratitude that I had a friend coming to me. I told her we had very little to offer. She told me she had nothing to offer. "See you when you get here. I can't wait to get my arms around you."

When they pulled into the driveway of the Rock House, their kids piled out of their borrowed car and peeled to the side with our kids, all quickly honed in on how to have fun together. We met Joseph and Lindsey in the yard and landed with our arms wrapped around, our tears mixed up on each other's faces. They've always been the kind of friends who don't know any better. They don't know how not to be close.

Joseph was the son of former missionaries to France, and so we teased him, called him "Frenchy." Lindsey grew up in a strong ministry family and had longed for the mission field for as long as she could remember. They had been lifelong believers in global ministry, had sought to fulfill their desire to be successful global workers. Yet, their experience abroad had nearly taken the life right out of them. To hug them was to feel the weight of it.

All that evening we sat so close that our knees touched. We held our plates in our laps and filled our glasses with wine. We interrupted each other and circled back into our stories, weaving in, exposing wounds, stopping for loss of words and picking back up in waves on the time line.

At the end of the evening, we bowed our heads to pray because this had been the culture of our friendship years before, and our need for healing in community brought us wordless to a God so palpable that all we did was sit and cry. All we could say was, "We are broken and you are here."

And at the end of the evening, we said let's do this again in a few days, and we did. Then again, we met, we ate, we prayed, and we decided to invite our other dear friends who had recently come home from a different missions assignment in Asia. So the six of us met, and one from the new couple didn't know what she believed of Jesus anymore, but we ate and we drank and we prayed our wordless prayers anyhow.

We were three couples, each of whom had lost its fit, and this being broken and bowing to simply contemplate the presence of God was the most holy community experience I had ever had. It was clear to me that he was with us. They were slow to see it, but I could see. It was as close as I had ever been to home, to see Christ in my friends, though I hardly saw him in myself. We were all heartbroken, but we found our small places in living rooms and on front porches. We found our places in silence and in laughter. We found that when three tiny food budgets combine, you can have exquisite meals.

It didn't take us long to learn that food and burdens and time were meant to be shared. Seth and I still had Africa in our hearts, and we didn't know how to handle it, but we wanted to make a way to be smaller still. All we knew was to be small. Joseph and Lindsey had moved to an apartment, and another apartment became available across the courtyard from them. We immediately found renters for the Rock House and moved to those apartments to be with them. Maybe that would bring us home. Slowly, slowly, with nights on our porches, over board games, and while co-mothering, I saw healing in my friends, and that was life enough for me.

In the apartments, the spaces were small, and the kids were a ruckus. The socks and underwear mixed up in the Laundromat. Any business we had was known throughout the building. You couldn't walk to your car without reporting to several people where you were going. Our neighbors were just as likely to get our pink notice for an unpaid bill as they were to hear us yell at our kids. There was a new smallness about us. At first, we were learning to know who we were in the quiet with God, and then we were learning who we were in the muck of actual community.

I had a three-year-old, a four-year-old, and a six-year-old when out of nowhere, I wanted to birth another baby. I knew it was crazy, but desire is desire. Within just a few minutes of taking yet another pregnancy test, I had walked over to Lindsey's apartment to show her the two pink lines. Then she watched me expand. She was already pregnant again herself, so we grew together. With our bellies out front and a laundry basket held to the side, we waddled to the washing machines with our sacks full of quarters and kids following behind us. The bigger we got, the less we did laundry and the more closed off we became.

At one point, Lindsey suggested that I at least open my window blinds to let the sun shine in. I could see her walk in from the parking lot below, her ankles all swollen. It was her time, and then her Nora was born, her third girl, a natural breech birth. Days later, Lindsey called from exhaustion, and I crossed the sidewalk to fetch Nora. I swaddled her and brought her to my rocking chair, the one set up for my new baby. Lindsey showered and took a nap, and I rocked and sang. These are the things you don't realize are making you who you are. Oh, the daughters I shared with our friends.

Then Arkansas got angry August-hot, and I hunkered down away from people as much as possible, but this didn't stop the boys from getting lice and sharing it with every other kid in the complex. I was huge, hot, and scared of ruining my baby because of chemicals. Seth shaved their heads, and I did a bunch of hippie stuff, such as using essential oil and mayonnaise, and kept doing loads and loads of laundry. This is also when Ian got chicken pox. Life was steamrolling me flat. Big as I was, I felt like I was being folded into a pill box, like the apartment was shrinking. I had contractions that interrupted me every day for weeks, and I learned to ignore my own pain. I have always been one to ignore or fall into despair. Once I couldn't ignore them anymore, the switch flipped, and I figured I had landed in perpetual August and I would be pregnant forever. I knew then that I would write this book, and at the end of it, I was still going to be large, angry, and hot.

I was sprawled out in my bed having contractions when I heard a familiar pop, but this time, instead of rushing out of bed, I ignored it. Nothing was happening. I called Seth an hour later and said, "Maybe come home and see me," though I wasn't convinced it was labor. He walked in and I apologized for making him come home for no reason, but then a contraction hit, and I went directly down on my hands and knees. When it was over, I said, "Go on back to work. This isn't the real thing." He just laughed and made me call the midwife. "Okay. Okay," I said to her, "I'll come in, and you can check me."

To get up on her table took some effort, and whatever effort I exerted must have been the last straw for the waters, because . . . her poor shoes. That did it. "Okay, fine. I'm in labor."

The big waves came quickly for this one. I was thrown in deep before I believed I was anywhere near the water. I called Brooke and Lindsey. This labor was a moaner. I never got my head around it. I never believed. I was terrified. Seth called another friend to send Bible verses about having no fear. As Seth read them aloud, I clung to them like buoys. If he paused, I would groan, "Read!" As I sat on my exercise ball, Brooke and Lindsey took turns countering back labor. I was going under. I thought I would sink.

Lindsey said again and again, "You're doing it, Amber. You're doing it." Then I had the urge to push, and as the day turned to night, the midwife walked in just in time to lift my gown. The Christmas song "Breath of Heaven" played, and Titus came right out into the midwife's arms. I said, "Oh! I did do it. We did it." Laughing. "I've seen this face three times before. A Haines boy!"

We had four boys, and Seth cracked open with joy. What a swing from disbelieving labor to the relief of a child born! The very metaphor of new life washed over us like a spotlight turning on, and we knew that every blink and crinkle was a precious thing. It was my most beautiful and trouble-free labor, and I knew as I panted and held him in my arms that if I had believed in my own body's ability to do the good thing God had made it to do, it would have given me so much less pain. I had believed through the pain for so many others, but I hadn't believed for myself. I had seen God in so many others. Being small had meant believing little good for myself. It had meant long-suffering with hope for others but despair for me.

When I held him in my arms, I decided in that moment to believe. Or I hoped to believe, at least. I knew then that I had exactly what I didn't know I wanted, a son. I had something within me that I didn't know I could really believe. It was a glimpse of completeness, of fighting fear, and of a cloud of witnesses saying, "You are complete in Christ." I wanted to be complete, but birthing children had not made it so. Scenes in a life are merely portals for understanding the greater thing, the invisible. And this, I was still learning.

Seeing my body do something beautiful gave me a peripheral glimpse of my own createdness, how I'm made, how I am the daughter birthed by very God. After the glimpse, I looked back on it as the birth of a mother who took on a new desire. I nursed through the night and thought of the distant thing that might satisfy me. *One day I will find myself in the wilderness again, and I will be unafraid.*

Sustain

Our small group of friends had begun with a long, silent pause like an orchestra before the music begins, like a cellist holding position with the bow hovering just above the strings.

We had learned to cram so many people into our apartment. We sat small on the floor, and we came hungry. We had gathered a group who had lived in close proximities to failure, last breaths, mental illnesses, warring children, and addiction. One grew up as the child of a missionary in China and held babies as they took their last breaths. Another had worked among the war-torn in Sarajevo and northern Uganda. There was a good boy, the son of a politician who'd experienced so much church trouble that it was a wonder he still believed in the church at all. There was one with a troubled marriage.

There was wide-eyed life too. College students with the world in front of them came, found life with us in the very real grit of life. And when we broke the bread and drank the wine, the words of milk and honey came into our prayers. This is when the silence let up and the bow touched down. This is when we began to sing.

Joseph and Lindsey's three girls and our four boys were a lot of sound for a small apartment, but we just kept adding to our numbers, and the married couples kept taking it biblically. We all went to the same big church, but these had become our family and had entered into life with us, and it was abundant and mysterious, a new, surprising movement here and there. We were full of life. Two more of the girls were pregnant. In fact, four of us had been pregnant at the same time for about a month.

Kaitlin's growing belly sat behind her guitar, and she was a waif otherwise with a pixie of black hair. She and Travis were young and unjaded. When she sang, it seemed impossible such sound could come from that mouth. Her voice came from her toes, and it moved us.

More and more, younger ones joined us to sing and know the joy of Christian community. Even some who didn't believe, or didn't want to be associated with Christians, came to be a part of it. There was a ragtag hope about the whole thing, no matter how cramped we got. The sound of joy is undeniable.

When one of us was able to cook a big meal, we would take part of it to another who didn't have the energy to stand and cook. *This is the kingdom of God*, we thought, and we were right. We gave each other glimpses of the kingdom in wine and spaghetti. The younger ones who weren't yet married spent such time taking care of us that they weren't lacking in what we knew of leadership. But still, we never meant to lead, and they never meant to have so many kids hanging on them or to fold so many of our clothes. It's just what happens when you spend time with people. There was nothing rigged about it.

There were little moments when I would look across to Lindsey and say, "This isn't going to last forever," meaning that we had better soak it up, because it was good, and it felt temporary. None of us ever assumed that we would live in our town for our whole lives. We knew we all happened to be journeying along at the same time, phase, and place. We were in a rare phase of learning how to be both common and uncommon.

One night, a friend from our little group hugged my neck and whispered, "You are a child of God." That's not something that normal people do. It's not normal to get together for a birthday and to end it in a baptism, but we did that too.

Part of the beauty was how awkward we all were, how willing we were to see a barrier and then to bust it down. If a heart was broken, Joseph had no problem walking straight for the ache and laying his hands on a shoulder. There's no way to know how many times, in the middle of boisterous laughter and conversation, we would sense a need, pause, and pull a chair to the center. We could be going ninety-to-nothing and then silent and into prayer.

Our Jared and Lindi had a big, furry, blue-eyed dog who shed more than the trees in autumn, and at the end of Lindi's pregnancy, we sneaked into their house and scrubbed it down. We cleaned the bathroom and hand-washed the dishes, and we hunted dog hair for two hours. Never had we smiled more. This was the kingdom. To be able to do anything for Lindi, one with a laugh born straight out of the belly of God, was to do oneself a favor. To serve with that small group was simple, and it was our joy. There's a "not yet, but already" about the people of God. We scrubbed house together, even though everything just gets dirty again.

When Travis and Kaitlin joined us, he had recently cut off his dreadlocks, which I'm sure had made him look like a tough cookie, but the truth of the matter was that his tender heart was made to burden bear. He was made to cry for joy and to cry just any time at all. We loved him so much. Once he came into the group, we all cried all the time, but not in the sad way. We kept each other tender and choked up. We lived as if we were loved, as if we had been touched by something much bigger than we were.

Kaitlin's pregnancy wasn't an easy one. Throughout her pregnancy, her platelet count continued to drop and drop. It was dangerously low, and I was terrified as she went into labor. The doctors had warned that such a low platelet count could lead to an inability to clot, which could cause her to bleed to death after delivery. We held vigil in prayer, and she and that baby Eliot did beautifully. They were healthy, though all medical staff had been put on high alert.

And if a normal delivery hadn't been enough, she and Travis experienced another miracle. We all did. They had no insurance at the time. Our group secretly gathered money and called individually to pay their bills as we could, and I guess the hospital got so aggravated by our calls that they forgave the remaining 90 percent of their bill.

The entire time we were thinking, *This is it! This is the whole thing! This is why we're on this planet.* Imagine the conductor of a symphony, his baton waving vigorously while the other hand opens palm up and the fingers ripple, "More, more, more!" In those days with our small group of friends, we were fully aware of the crescendo of our beautiful lives. We thought we had found the kingdom come.

We crammed so much life into our little houses and apartments that we felt like a secret place from the world. We went to Sunday morning church and would think, *Wow, you clean up nice*, when during the week, we would see the paper piles, strewn toys, and dishes piled up in the sink. They were the sweatpants friends who kept us in the ease of leftovers.

Though heartache was always present, in that sweet phase we were beautiful. Our culture was beautiful. I told stories to my boys, and one particular story of Jesus got caught in Isaac's throat. He had a hard time swallowing it. Jesus died. He couldn't get over it, so he came to us and asked if he could be baptized. "If the Ethiopian eunuch got baptized immediately, then why wouldn't I?"

Our friends surrounded us the day Seth baptized his firstborn son. Travis gave Isaac a new journal, and throughout were snippets of his own past journals. He copied photos from Uganda and pasted words he had written when he had lived there so Isaac would know what it looked like to contemplate God in beauty and in pain.

When Jared and Lindi's firstborn was dedicated at church, they gave us a letter and a tiny gift that I keep with my pearls in the jewelry box. It is a treasure that I will pray for that child until the day I die. I will remember the meaning of his name ("servant warrior"), and I will go about my life believing that he will one day bind up the brokenhearted. That is what his parents did for me.

We had all birthed four babies in eight months, and so it was suddenly time to get back into the Rock House. They helped us move, and we were grateful to have a larger place to meet. All I imagined for the Rock House then was a dining room full of people, food, and singing. This time, it would be home with my four boys. This time, we would be complete.

Because my first three were born in three years, I had only experienced having a bunch of babies at once. They were all playing together as soon as they could communicate, but none of them were taking care of each other. When Titus was born, that had all changed. He had three big brothers doting. Three boys offered to bring me the pacifier or the diapers. Isaac could actually rock him for me. It was a new experience, and I felt it all as a gift, as a mystery unfurling.

During his first weeks in the apartment, Titus breathed like one running a marathon. Our apartment bedroom was lined tight with furniture, and I crawled in from the foot of the bed. His full lips perched open in a smirk. Even as a newborn, he slept with one eye half open, afraid he might miss something, keeping the energy of someone who loves fun. He slept deep and still breathed like his heart was ready to jump out of his body. It turned out that he had a hole in his heart that wouldn't affect him too much, but before we knew that, one of our elders' wives prayed that he would "grow to be a man of strong heart." I knew in the moment that this would be my prayer for his life. The name Titus is associated with the words "pleasing," "defender," and "giant." In my mother prayers, I foresaw him as such, a pleasant protective giant with a huge heart.

Titus was born full-term and as healthy as could be, yet by the time he was six months old, we knew his body was struggling to fight infections. It took us weeks to find the correct antibiotics to treat an abscessed lymph node. I didn't realize that for a few months after that, he had not gained an ounce. When we began keeping watch on his weight, feeding him coconut oil and every fattening thing, we realized he was losing weight instead.

The doctors decided to watch him in the hospital. My mother-in-law came right away, and our little group of friends rallied strong and let worry be no option. We were in the hospital for three days forcing calories, and I was as exhausted as I had ever been up to that point. During those three days, he gained weight, and we thought it was over.

A few days later, I could tell he wasn't well, so I called my girlfriend who is also his pediatrician, and she told us to come in the back door of the office. We got to see leftover birthday cake on a side table and peek into the real-life world of doctors with cubicles full of photographs of their own children. The medical world mostly freaks me out, and I would have rather gone to see a hippie in the vitamin aisle than gone back to that hospital, but she's such a friend, and I trust her. Titus lay naked, all grins, on the scales, and I knew he hadn't grown, but it showed he had lost a pound, as if we had never spent those days in the hospital. I had all the boys with me and called Seth to meet us in a procedure room so we could learn together how to insert a feeding tube for home.

I had never seen one, but it was a simple tube that went up his nose and into his tummy. I would stick what looked like a turkey baster to the end of it and pump in the needed formula. Without the tube, his health teetered on a nosedive.

We met with our friends, and I finally cried. Brothers hugged me, and sisters wrapped their arms around my legs and sat with me. One sobbed into my ear.

In the Rock House, we were supposed to be passing plates around our table and gathering others to the center for prayer, but instead we hosted only those who came to serve us. Titus had begun to wither. He was throwing up his tube feedings. Our guy friends would take the older boys down to the creek, while I sat and listened to the air conditioner work summer-hard. I felt carried outside of my own body.

Titus continued to vomit everything that entered his body, and so we revisited the doctors, but they had exhausted their options. They called Arkansas Children's Hospital in Little Rock and made arrangements for our immediate admission. As I was leaving the doctor's office in shock, thinking of all the things that needed to happen in a short time to get us out of town, I saw Joseph waiting outside for me with a cup of coffee.

After I pulled into our driveway, Emily played with our older boys, and the rest of the group descended on us with bags of groceries and a weed eater. One immediately started on our lawn. One cleaned out our refrigerator because we would be gone awhile. I never would have thought of that. One came with a medical notebook with files and tabs so I could organize my thoughts and keep up with what the doctors would be sharing with us. They packed us up and prayed us out of the driveway. I still didn't know how to get back inside my own body. I hardly knew who I was.

Rich Mullins and King David sang us all the way to Little Rock. All the black hills rolled us forward, like we were following whole, slow notes on a full scale. Praying that Titus would just get well, I wondered about whether or not I hunger and thirst for righteousness. What would sustain me?

My sister-in-law met us at the emergency room in Little Rock to take the big boys with her. One cried and buckled himself back into our van, not wanting us to leave him. It was pitch dark out, and all we knew were the hospital lights shining up ahead.

There was a deep breath, a comma, an inhale before we took the walk in alone. The stars were singing. Moments of unknowing and waiting are keen moments. One foot in front of the other, with our baby in our arms, we walked in holy awareness.

Muscle Memory

My clothes were hanging neatly to the side, and on a table with a lit candle, a tiny bowl held my wedding rings and necklace. It had been six weeks since the hospital, and the knots in my shoulders and back held me wonky to the side. I couldn't turn my neck to the right or the left, so I called a masseuse, and before the end of the day, she had my feet soaking in hot water. She was an older woman, had made a red hibiscus iced tea, and she smelled like my mama. I wore a robe she gave me, sat in an upright chair, closed my eyes, sipped tea, and listened to soft music with birds chirping in the background.

When the woman came in, she bowed to her knees at the steaming bowl. She picked up each foot and gently washed it like a mama. She asked questions from there, from the floor. She massaged my calves with my wet feet held against her broad legs.

When I had answered her questions, she left the room for me to get on the massage table facedown. Back in the room, she folded the blanket back and exposed me. I had already told her of our time in the hospital. She already knew. As she worked her thumbs into my shoulders, I cried so many tears that the floor beneath my face was wet. It wasn't the pain so much that made me cry. I supposed her to have the gift of healing. It was her hands altogether. It was an unexpected and foreign intimacy that I hadn't allowed myself, the intimacy that comes with being the child. With the touch of a mother, she was a stranger whose love was beyond us both.

She spoke no words except these: "Muscles have memories. You may have dealt in your mind with how hard it was to be in the hospital with your Titus, but muscles have memories too. They don't forget as easily as we want."

What I'm saying is, she gave a good massage.

❧

They were supposed to be expecting us at Arkansas Children's Hospital but weren't, so we went in through the emergency room, knowing they would keep him. We finally got a room at 3:30 a.m. and slept for two hours before a team of doctors was assigned to Titus. He still couldn't keep his food down, and the following days were a blur of needles and scans, cycles of doctors and interns and lab technicians. Not once did a nurse get an IV in him on the first try, and then some days he just ripped it out. We repeatedly withheld food, even when he was hungry, because he had to undergo so many procedures and couldn't eat for twelve hours prior. He had his first colonoscopy, upper GI with biopsies, full body scans, and MRIs.

Seth and I slept in chairs for two solid weeks while nurses intermittently woke us all to take Titus's blood pressure, pulse, and sugar levels. Every time they woke Titus, we had to rock him back to sleep. They weighed him every morning at 5:30 a.m. Our bodies took on the kind of ache only known by watchmen without relief. That's what we had become. It was a careful job to know his body enough to predict when he wouldn't keep his food down. It was a careful job to hold him calm and to tell the self to just do the next thing. Parts of my body and mind began to feel robotic, while my awareness for Titus was heightened, as if to strengthen one thing I had to let all the other things go. I tapped into Titus by disassociating with all other parts of myself. All my desires rerouted into him and his health.

Titus, on the other hand, didn't have a care in the world. He had no idea that we weren't there simply to hold him for Kung-Fu-Panda time. That child oozed happy and fun, and his desire to make someone smile couldn't even be starved out of him. Even when the doctors decided to stop his feeds altogether, even when his body wasn't accepting food at all, he smiled. They walked in expecting a darkness and then checked the charts to make sure they had the right room. They fell in love with him, celebrating half ounces and bringing him gifts. The child never understood that he was sick.

I kept thinking about our previous Sunday at church, how all I could repeat in prayer was, "I don't want to break. I don't want to break." After telling a friend about my weariness, she said, "Maybe that's exactly what you're supposed to do—let yourself break." One of my greatest fears was losing my mind, my understanding, and my faith. One of my greatest fears was that I would reorient so much that I would question God's goodness. I told myself that if I broke, I would never make it. I knew I wasn't the one in whom all things hold together, and yet I wasn't free to tremble. I couldn't break.

Then there was the night that swung like a hinge between two parts of a life, between everything before and everything after. Titus had thrown up all his meals from afternoon through the night, and his glucose levels plummeted. It was 4:45 a.m., and his body was limp. We had been awake all night. We were confused. The doctors rushed him out for something I can't remember. When they returned him to me, his sugar levels had gone back up. I held his worn-out body and wept. I talked to God. I said words like "glory." I said words like "trust." I said, "No matter what," but I didn't know what I meant.

I rocked and considered the songs we would play at his funeral.

I had not been in a stage of great Scripture consumption. I had not prayed without ceasing, but the night we thought Titus was dying was the night I cracked. Part of me felt held with hands, and part of me was blown back in fear, as if God threatened to fill me like a roar of molten lava. Weak places are indeed a siphon for glory. I sat in a place I could hardly bear like a vessel cracking under pressure. *Will I break? Can I contain this kind of pain? Can I let God have this child? Do I have a choice?*

Then I heard the voice of peace, as if God had settled in the next room over. I knew he was there and experienced his comfort peripherally, but the inner realm, the intimate dimension made for dwelling in peace, was not an open place. I couldn't break. Fear sealed me from allowing such intimacy. Peace was a thing I believed in, just over in the glory land, like a gift I could open when I die. I couldn't allow it in, yet peace still somehow filtered my fear of losing a child and turned it into a temporary thing. I was swallowed up in fear but knew it would be over soon. Belief in heaven does this. I jerked back, as far as I could with a cracked heart, but in the moment, peace swooped in and surrounded us from outside of time. I rocked my baby, and in the rocking chair we were eternal.

Then I closed my eyes and took a morning nap with Titus stretched out on my chest. When day broke, all the doctors looked confused and called him a mystery, a puzzle. After so many days of this, his genius, loving, and highly qualified team was at a loss and had several meetings to discuss a new course. They changed his feedings to drop by drop through his feeding tube—continuous feeding.

He was to receive 40 mls of elemental formula an hour for four hours. At the end of that period, they were to remove residual fluids from his tummy. We found out that his feedings were not passing through his stomach, at least not as quickly as they should, so the slower we gave him food, the more he was able to process it. By the next morning, he had gained weight. We found that he could digest only an ounce of food an hour. We never figured out why.

It apparently only takes a little to give Titus what he needs to prove what a bruiser he is. One morning, surrounded by doctors, he was overcome with playfulness and jumped from his bed toward us all, as if he might fly. Instead of flying, he busted his eye and bled everywhere before outwrestling four nurses as they put a butterfly Band-Aid above his eyebrow.

Titus is his perfect name, a paradox that doesn't add up. He's a big-hearted child in a tiny body. They had him on the WHO Protocol for malnutrition, and we talked about him in terms used in third world countries. We used the phrases "failure to thrive" and "starvation mode" while sitting in one of the best children's hospitals in the world, where Santa Claus walked in for "Christmas in July" with a huge bag of toys just for Titus.

I couldn't get anything to add up. Intake of calories never equaled weight gain. America never equaled good health. My work never equaled enough. I didn't know how to pray, but I never questioned God's love, because I was consumed in it for Titus. Mother love is born of God. I kept a smile along with my ache as I worked in that love. This was the place I became a giver, but I never turned mother love on its side to see that I could receive it. That's the world I was coming to know, the world that didn't add up.

After two weeks, we checked out of the hospital with no idea what was wrong with Titus. We accidentally found that he had chiari malformation, and he did have inflammation, but after two weeks with some of the world's greatest minds, we only knew to continue tube feeds to get him to gain.

When we pulled in the driveway, I saw a blue bird flit across the yard, the crispy grass a perfect backdrop. I noticed how good the sunshine was and how good it was to see life in contrast. My breast milk was almost dry and all the food in the world wasn't enough for Titus, but there were good things stacked in the mail and tomatoes to pick.

Before we left for the hospital, I felt somehow that I might be in shock. The words "failure to thrive" and "starvation mode" in association with my own child didn't move me like my brain told me they should. I was holding the words but not accepting them. I was inside my body watching it move.

Isaac yelled from way up in the tree, and Jude ran to me screaming, "Emergency! Emergency!" I went out to see my oldest floating in brittle vines three stories over my head. I shook all over and felt the pressure build as I acclimated again to life with four sons. I talked him down. The suckle was parched in drought. Fear of the break knotted into my memory. I feared they would fall. I feared they would slip through my hands like undrunk water. I feared what I would make of the time I had.

For weeks, Titus's weight yo-yoed. We slowly upped his feeds, and overall he gained with every increase through the pump. So many friends came to my aid that I didn't sweep my own kitchen floor for maybe a month. My sister and sister-in-law planned to come and help, but we asked them to wait. All I wanted was the normal back. I didn't want the help. I wanted to sweep and scrub dried applesauce off the linoleum. I would have done anything to have the old way back again, but everything rolled forward. Time was a line moving my body and our beautiful lives straight ahead, while parts of me rocked back and forth on a hinge in my memory, a rocking chair back in Little Rock.

Titus turned one the day after we returned home from the hospital, and we had an impromptu birthday party for him and Jude, since Jude had turned six while we were away. Only two weeks after all that chaos, Jude started kindergarten. I wanted to hold his hand for one week straight. And during that time, no one had taught Ian a single thing. He was dressing himself and zipping his pants up the back. Yet he could somehow say all his letters.

Isaac started second grade, and I wondered if I had skipped second grade because I couldn't remember it, which may be a good thing since I had never faked confidence more than when I sent my own kids off to school. I fidgeted through the universal smell of elementary school hallway and hated the anxiety. I hated the back and forth of trust and doubt, of being here but far away.

For our stage of life, the chaos was perfectly normal. We were pushing through, doing the next thing, and as we pushed, desire was leaving my body. Titus's health stayed the same and couldn't uphold my desire any longer.

At the market square splayed with late summer, I wrapped my senses in ripe tomatoes, hot banjos, and exposed tattoos. The broad smiles of a planting day told me that relief was on its way, rain even. I saw it with my eyes. Everything bent burnt orange, life gone out from us. Titus kicked his happy legs, and I was pushing him in a stroller with a bag of ripe peaches dangling from the handles. They smelled so good.

He still had that feeding tube as we edged autumn, and I didn't think about it until I saw heads turn. They said, "Look how precious," and I saw that they wanted to ask what was wrong, what disease would require a tube to snake up a baby's nose. I just mentioned those new apples. "Are they sour?" A boy played mandolin. An old man had a wrinkled puppy on a leash. We folded to the ground to pet her. In late summer, the corner of the square was ripe and rich, a rainbow of fragrances, everyone facing the music.

Some from our church had told me that God doesn't design our bodies with faults. Some called what was happening in Titus a work of the devil. I heard the battle cry of how we're made for Eden, for wholeness, and I agreed with so much of it, that Titus was made to walk with God, but maybe not like all these armchair theologians thought. I saw Titus, sick, but not the work of the devil. He was my baby, more whole than I felt.

It took me ten minutes to load up the van. Apples rolled across the parking lot, and Titus fussed. I didn't know if he would eat at all, but I saw no devil there. I ate a peach and called my day good as I walked our time line like a tightrope, still outside of my body, still seeing God in it all as from another room over.

Members of our good church laid their gentle hands on our heads and begged our faith to move this mountain. My family church from Alabama prayed more than monks ringing bells.

During one naptime, his feeding tube came out and pumped all his milk into the bed. I held my hands up and said, "Do what you will with my children. Take them or heal them." I didn't know how to pray. I begged no specifics, only general glory. If Titus's delays became pronounced, what would that mean of God then? What of his special needs, the boy who introduced me to so much of my own inborn weakness? The church can tend to treat the beautiful and privileged ones like they have a corner on God's goodness. Is a life more because it's long, less because it's short? A healthy 20/20 vision doesn't mean the eyes of our hearts can see. We weren't made to desire perfect health on this earth.

When you touch the knots in my shoulders and neck, pray for future memory. Prophesy me Eden. Pray me a vision of home. Imagine Titus there, a strong man, heart soaring, because his eyes are open to God—because he knew the intimacy of love.

Seed of Desire

But each person is tempted when he is lured and enticed by his own desire. Then desire when it has conceived gives birth to sin, and sin when it is fully grown brings forth death. Do not be deceived, my beloved brothers. Every good gift and every perfect gift is from above, coming down from the Father of lights with whom there is no variation or shadow due to change. Of his own will he brought us forth by the word of truth, that we should be a kind of firstfruits of his creatures. Know this, my beloved brothers: let every person be quick to hear, slow to speak, slow to anger; for the anger of man does not produce the righteousness of God. Therefore put away all filthiness and rampant wickedness and receive with meekness the implanted word, which is able to save your souls. But be doers of the word, and not hearers only, deceiving yourselves. For if anyone is a hearer of the word and not a doer, he is like a man who looks intently at his natural face in a mirror. For he looks at himself and goes away and at once forgets what he was like. But the one who looks into the perfect law, the law of liberty, and perseveres, being no hearer who forgets but a doer who acts, he will be blessed in his doing.

James 1:14–25 ESV

Right before Seth finished law school, just as my belly and rear end began to round out with our first child, we took a beach vacation to south Florida where buxom women tend to forget their tops. It was the first time we vacationed together, and because of my growing ways and all the boobs on the beach, the entire thing centered around food, what to eat, how to get to the food, how much the food would cost, and how long it would take before we could eat again. I had honest-to-goodness key lime pie, the memory of which still makes my eyes roll to the back of my head.

We spent some time in Miami and had heard of a restaurant that offered the very best in Cuban food, and it was the thing I had looked forward to the most about the entire week. We drove through what felt like a different, spicier country of exotic limes and beautiful skin, and an hour went by before Seth confessed that we were lost. This was before cell phones took over being smart for us, and once I saw the backside of some shady shipping crates for the fourth time and then a real-life Black Panther member wearing a beret and standing guard at a warehouse door, I began to weep. I was not crying because I was scared about where we were. I don't get scared of people very easily, and the truth is there's not a fear on this planet that can compare to the raging hunger of a pregnant woman who has long imagined authentic fried plantains and Cuban black beans. I would have marched straight through any ghetto for something to eat, would have asked a pack of Black Panthers for directions. I was so hungry that I bawled, fully convinced that my baby was eating my brain and there wasn't much left, and so therefore we would both starve to actual death within thirty minutes.

We had been near the hole-in-the-wall restaurant we were looking for the entire time. We finally found it and parked next to a light pole. My head was throbbing so that I could hear my heart beating in my ears, and I lunged out in my little skirt, without caring who I flashed. I held myself up on that light pole, made some calculations, didn't bother with Seth, and found my way toward the first person I saw with a pad of paper and a pencil. I didn't care who she was as long as she took my order to whoever the cook was.

The thing is there wasn't a soul there who could speak English. I'm afraid it's possible that I called out, "Somebody help me!" and if I did, the Lord must have heard me. I hadn't taken Spanish in five years, and I had squeezed through those courses by the hair of my chin. This, somehow, didn't matter, because my child was killing off his own host by siphoning everything good out of me, and I was on the verge of walking straight to the kitchen to find a ladle and a bowl.

This is the first time I spoke in tongues. It had to have been tongues because I can't tell how it happened except that desire made it so. I clearly told that woman to get me a chair and please, dear mercy, bring me the first thing she could find that

I could shove down my throat. I said it all in Spanish, and I would translate it for you right now, except I don't know how. When she brought me those syrupy, hot, fried plantains on a paper plate, I looked at her with the gratitude of one whose life had clearly been saved.

This is what I know of desire. Desire affects the whole person, mind, body, and soul. Desire is a drive. It is a hunger that opens its mouth. It is a dissatisfaction, a longing, a wintered beast of prey. It is the hand of Potipher's wife for Joseph's coat. It is madness for the harp of David.

When we returned from the hospital with Titus, all my desire had gathered up in a great spitting fire against his illness, but after some time, it died a little and turned a plume of pitch. After months and months of no answers, desire went the way of hope, as it always does. Once in a while, smoke would rise from me, as when a city falls but hasn't yet let go of its breath.

A year after we came home from the hospital, I was living my new mode of survival, my new normal, an unhinged whirlwind, and I was still finding ways our community had blessed us. It was many months later that I looked up and realized that my books on the shelf had all been alphabetized while we were gone. I cried at how precious they had been to us, and the sweetness made the isolation sting. Our group had made the decision to divide because we kept multiplying, and we couldn't fit into anybody's house anymore. We were supposed to be leading one of the three groups, but Seth and I both left the hospital in such a thick cloud that we lacked the sense to lead anyone anywhere, except maybe into despair.

Titus's health stayed the same, in a teetering limbo, and we backed out of community for recovery that took much longer than we expected. During the time we had allowed for healing, we couldn't see through the fog. We isolated ourselves. We couldn't see what it was we needed.

I was able to feed and clothe my children. I read to them once in a while, and then all my energy went into keeping them alive. I heard them discuss how to get on the roof to swing to the nearest tree. I heard them discuss what it would taste like to mix bird poop with mud. One time I walked into the kitchen, smelled gas from the stove, and yelled at everyone to get to the carport. From there, one told me there was a fire in the garbage can. He had caught paper on fire from the stove, blown the stove out, and then trashed the lit paper. I had literally made it my job to put out small fires.

I lived on edge. I wrinkled my face tight in efforts not to gasp when I heard a thump, and life with four sons can seem nothing but thumps. There were so many things to tune out that I had to have something to tune in to. During the year after Titus's hospital experience, I went deep into planning new living arrangements for yet another move. Someone wanted to buy our house, and it became my chance to make home.

When the nice fellow from Texas contacted us and asked if he could buy the Rock House without our having listed it, something in us gave a huge sigh of relief. *Oh yes, indeed, we would love to get out of here.* This sweet couple wanted in there to give the Rock House some new life. The wife glowed with ideas. I wanted to warn them that if another doorknob came off in my hands, they might have to move in and repair the old melty looking window I had chunked the knob through.

A new move gave me something to lean toward, somewhere to focus my desire. I ordered four side tables, two couches, two rugs, and so many others things that I had to sell the dining room table to fit all the boxes in the dining room before the move. This of course meant I needed a new dining room table too, and probably chairs.

When I heard a huge crash and three boys yelling, it broke me from my stupor. They had been running circles around me in the living room to a well-worn path through my bedroom and had knocked over a huge mirror and broken it. I was numb and deep inside my online lists for a better life when I heard the crash and jerked myself up through the wires and out of the screen. In a flash, I embodied such fear and frustration, the sound of shattered glass echoing through me, that I ran into the room shaking violently. Everyone was fine. Everything was fine, but I handled a broom and dustpan in such a rage that I caused more terror in the boys that day than if a thousand mirrors had broken.

When the crash woke me up, I woke up to pain, and I didn't like it. My imagination was a place to go, like a gin and tonic or a lover. I was living as a pretend version of myself so I didn't have to face the pain of having a child who wouldn't heal or a community that couldn't provide a permanent fit. Underneath the move and the planning was an anger at a rolling boil, and to be disrupted was to burn the ones I loved. My desire was to disappear. How many tiptoes walked around me then?

❧

In Eden, the flowers dripped with life, and all the vibrant petals opened to Eve. Everything was in its richest form, reaching always to the good sun, drinking waters in newest circulation, and bearing fruit. Barefooted, she walked with God and her only man. Think of every part, how available.

There was the one thing she wanted that she couldn't have, and her want grew inside her how a thing does before it is born and takes on a life of its own. As it was born, it propelled its way forward with the inertia of any other birth. Forward, the hand reached and broke the fruit from the tree. Everything became involved then, her lips, the inside of her, a rush of knowledge to every part: *I am woman. I am good. I am evil.* Born from her desire was an action that led to her very death.

This is the way of sin. The fruit of its desire does not lead to life. It does not lead to love, joy, peace, patience, kindness, goodness, faithfulness, gentleness, or self-control.[1] This is how we know the difference between a desire that leads to death and one implanted by the Father of lights, who gives every good and perfect gift. The fruit always tells.

If perfect love casts out fear,[2] it is safe to say that any desire born out of fear is not a desire that leads to love or life. Fear divides us from within, and so how is it possible to "love the LORD your God with all your heart and with all your soul and with all your strength"[3] if we are divided and motivated by fear?

When the fog and fear of grief landed on me the year after the hospital, I became fractured in a way that kept me from loving with my whole self, and without the whole self, I didn't have the sense to check my desires, to know what fruits my desires were growing. One from the other (wife from husband, mother from sons) and one from within (mind from body from soul), we fracture. It was like backward walking for us during those days, a process of un-recovery. Seth topped off his gin and tonics in secret. I loomed in shopping carts as a way to tap into another world, a way to inject a sense of hope. I counted pennies and bought clothes and art and arranged an imagined life of control and order and clarity while my boys ran unanswered circles around me. I planned and spent our money as if I were buying sanity. Maybe I could buy myself home, where guilt wasn't swallowing me so, keeping me strung up in anger.

Deeper into the bottle and deeper into my to-do lists and imaginary occasions to wear beautiful clothes, we engaged ourselves in an undoing, and with every undoing (the drinks, the shopping, the disappointed stomp), I entered deeper inside myself, desire so muddy I didn't know I wasn't whole. I didn't know I oozed rage and isolated myself because of it. I didn't know believers could live in a constant, shirking retreat of the soul.

I had refused to be broken, but all along I had walked around in pieces. I didn't want to be alone, but all along I had cut off the people who loved me most. Like a child mad at being told to wait, I didn't want to ask anything more from God, not a single thing. I always treat the church how I believe the Father treats me. Cutting off communion with him meant cutting off from his people. Instead of reaching out as a hurting part of the whole body, I turned inward. I shopped and craved, desired and bought in. I was buying a kingdom brick by brick, and at the top, I would see clearly, my tower built by endless imaginations of a complete, beautiful, and answered life. I was so overcome with wanting because I wasn't living as my whole self, how I was made to reach out, how I was made to feel deeply and to be loved.

I considered the metaphors of life the entire point of living, the metaphors of marriage and motherhood and community. I had no idea how to stop. The more I wanted completion in those metaphors, the more I divided internally and separated myself from Seth and the boys, from God. The angrier I became without an answer for Titus, the more I refused to give an answer to community and the more the boys begged me to look up in attention. This is how normal life looked to me, like addiction again, idolatry, like a body not knowing where her mind is and a mind not believing its own soul.

Every desire within me was cutting me three ways, mind from body from soul, breaking me down. The fruit of my desire was rage, anxiety, isolation, and exhaustion.

Our rhythms were interrupted in full stops, pocked with begging. "Titus, please eat." "God, make him gain." Tiniest pieces of me smoldered. I thought of prayer, remembered peace. Every day I was thinner, a divided self, working as a fraction of myself in weakest order. What else is there to do but strengthen oneself the only way she knows how?

I sat for hours and hours making lists. I listed foods Titus could eat. I scanned my schedule and wrote down every move

I would make. I wanted control of myself, the spiral within. I would make myself a life and put one foot in front of the other. The desire to survive created in me a striving I had never known. I was striving so hard that I had to lean into the kitchen counter to hold up my lungs. I couldn't catch my breath. I was working to breathe.

I added to the list: Try elimination diet. Buy expensive lotion. Make doctor appointments. Take antidepressants. Start more charts for the boys. Discipline us all. Get under control. And the more I added to the list, the less I accomplished. Every step of striving was a wall, a barrier against love. I wasn't even sad anymore. I was distracted. Every effort toward control made me more numb, and if you can't feel, you aren't alive anymore. Control was killing me. I had to think, *Breathe*, *check the pulse*, *balance*, *imagine*.

The inspector came to do the one last thing before we could close on our new house, before our buyers could get the loan, but then after the inspection, he disappeared and never turned in the inspection. The couple selling us their gorgeous house with two living rooms moved the day before closing, but our buyers still couldn't get their loan because of the man who disappeared. Our sellers gave up on us, so we lost the house that had become the foundation of my dreams. In fact, we lost two houses in the wait. Our boxes were completely packed for months, and this is when all the metaphors melted down, and I didn't know what anything meant anymore.

I got in the bed and stayed there. I cannot tell you how long. This was the thickest fog, the door shut, the covers up, the looking back on life and seeing meaninglessness. I had spent much of my life desiring beautiful things, considered most precious gifts from God, and yet I found myself incomplete. Not health or home, family or poetry, sex or systematic theology, no hiding place or child-birthing experience, not marriage or community or any good doing had put me together as a whole person. Not my role as daughter of Paul Carothers, wife of Seth Haines, mother of four amazing sons, or leader in the church had ever told me who I was in a way that found me complete. All my desire had wished it so, but the names, the metaphors given that point to God, were lackluster, never what I desired because (I see it now) the thing itself, the metaphor, is not God.

⚘

I am most alive when I am writing and when I am preaching. These are the ways I most hear from God, when I am intimately leaning in to his voice, his words. These are his good gifts to me, to hear his voice and to know that he is with me. I find intimacy with God this way.

In healthier seasons, these gifts gave me a fit into active church, and so I connected with other women with similar passions to make the name of Jesus known through their gifts. At my worst, my foggiest moment, I chose to do the most humiliating thing in a Facebook group of about sixty of these women, women I respected and women I desperately desired would see me as strong and capable. Because I had nothing left to lose, I spoke against my own fear of brokenness.

I don't remember exactly what I said, only that it was short. I mentioned having insecurities, and there would have been no way for those women to know how deep they went, how I questioned everything I thought I knew about myself. I was in a room of perceived spiritual giants, and I made my short cry for help, asked for prayer, and then backed out of the room fully expecting crickets and a few freshman back pats. I expected to be discounted, but what I got was Esther, whose very name suggests "for such a time as this."

Her response was a very simple thing, something close to "Do not forget that the Spirit of God indwells you." And just like that, with a word of truth, the ash blew over, and I began to burn.

It wasn't like lightning. It was a slow burn. *Holy Spirit? Who are you? Who are you in me?* And my questions pushed me forward, and I began to read. Do I have these gifts?[4] I had never claimed them. I had assumed many gifts for special men and a special fewer women, but certainly not for me. I can write it now, that writing and preaching are gifts, but until then, I hadn't received them that way. I hadn't done anything in a while that wasn't my own striving.

Scripture says in James that once desire is conceived it gives birth to sin, and then again James uses the same language of pregnancy when he says, "Receive with weakness the implanted word."[5] He goes on to explain that this leads to a life of doing, not merely hearing.[6] A seed always blooms into some sort of action.

This is the deep calling into the deep. Desire blooms in the soul, the hollow, like a womb, as a place intended for life, for growth, and for fruit. God's Word plants desire into our weakness, the fertile ground of brokenness, and that desire brings us forth as a people who live like Christ. His desire thrusts us forward in action, and we extend from him as life givers. We are of his very seed. We are a people born of him.

When Esther dropped a simple word into me, it settled like peace into my weakness, and I knew then that I could face my sadness and ask God about how debilitated I had been by the desire for control that held me hostage in bed. I had to ask him of my lust, what to do with the birth of sin. Acknowledging the Spirit in me was a conception. It was a reaching out reminiscent of Eve's desire toward the fruit, only this time the movement was for fruit that leads to life. Esther's words entered me with the inertia of light, and born was desire from God that overcomes. I felt the metaphor of being born again.

There is control that speaks in light, time, matter, and gravity. This is the control that can make it rain on the just and the unjust. This control makes the burning bush, a morning of manna, and the zygote dividing. The other kind of control is self-control, a gift born by the Spirit of God to help us walk in the narrow way of life and to say no to things that pull us aside. I had neglected the Spirit within me, the self-control given to me in him, and I had tried to claim control that wasn't even possible for me to have. Self-control is a rest in him and his way, and all other striving is an illusion of control that divided me in three, mind from body from soul. Dropping the illusion propelled me toward healing.

Habits need to heal too, and my mind habits were to spin wheels. My spirit was open and ready, but my thoughts were patterned in loops, and I was grateful for the traction that medication gave me to get out of the loops. Too many people feel guilty about the help of medicine, as if some demons weren't properly thwarted, but I have no problem or pride with seeing science working in the palm of God's hand. Part of my weakness has always been a tendency to get stuck, and for a brief time, medication helped me like putting a log under a tire that had been slinging mud. I got out of bed, and I was able to release control, see clearly, and move forward. The fruit always tells whether the action was right.

I was able to get up and see that my striving against sadness had driven me to despair. In those days of gaining traction and of remembering my gifts, I remembered the gift of suffering, of sharing in it with Christ,[7] and how I was actually made to live close to sadness, to bear up under the yoke, because that yoke is with my Jesus, the man of sorrows. To reject the shared suffering and sorrow with our Lord is to invite despair, and to walk as a burden bearer with him is to oppose despair. Sorrow is the very place that hope and joy intermingle, because without sorrow, there is no whisper of hope. Joy is a sustainer, the strength in weakness, and hope is what calls us forward toward our healing. In this world, we will have trouble,[8] but our great Peacemaker walks in the sorrow with us, and he is our joy. He is our peace. He is our hope. Sorrow does not overcome.

I look back on it all now, the affair, the anger, and the disappointment in church, and I see that my desire always followed my hope, the thing I thought would free me, and hope always propelled me forward. This time my hope was that my Jesus is a planter of good things and that he was growing me toward him. Of all the desirous ones, he is most desirous of me.

See Through

On our early morning flight, the attendant offered me a drink, and with every intense ounce of my being, I asked for coffee. I may have grunted it, because she and the woman on my left bent their bodies in a knee-slapping laugh right to my face. I laughed, too, and then had to explain that I was a decade tired in the mother way. I said, "I have four sons!"

"Oh!" the woman sitting there said. "I have three sons." And there it was, the look we gave each other, an immediate bond. She was from Joplin, Missouri, a place wiped out in 2011 by an EF5 tornado. I asked her how recovery was going, and she spoke of her dearest friends, how a light had gone out from their eyes. I saw the heartbreak as she wondered if she would ever see the light again.

How interesting it was to see an American woman's heart after she found herself and her community in the rubble. I was in the air on my way to Haiti, a place devastated by a catastrophic earthquake in 2010. I thought how familiar the rubble is to us all in varying degrees. I thought how some of us have looked death straight in the face, how some of us bow to death in overwhelming fear. How do we survive after such a thing?

When we finally sold our house, we had no house to purchase. Those opportunities had passed us by, and we were forced to learn that a house is not a good hope. If we wanted to experience hope, we couldn't shortcut to it, for hope is never without a wait. We sold some things and put others in storage. We had plans, money, and every material thing we needed, and yet we were homeless. Close friends were leaving town for the summer during our days without a home, and so we lived in their space, used their towels, played their records, and cooked from their stove. None of it was mine. The metaphor rang loud and clear. We were growing into health, spinning Neil Young, and resting on their back porch, and none of it was under my control. Even though Titus was still in limbo, I was living a new surrender, a new openness to the voice of God, a new hope. When leaning into the Spirit, it is not a process of mere hearing and then being okay. It is always an active work, a doing, but it is a work in conjunction. It is the work of receiving. It is the work of moving forward in intimacy and in rest.

I wanted to know the Spirit of God, and so I asked him to help me know and then to act on the knowledge. It was the only way I could be pulled out of my own head. Even though I was terrified of being associated with charismatics and had no idea what I was doing, I asked for every gift of the Spirit, especially the gift of prophecy, to see beyond, because Paul instructs us to seek that gift above all, even above preaching, discernment, and teaching.[1] No one seems to have done away with teaching, but prophecies have been used to manipulate and control. It's no wonder I grew up being taught that prophecy doesn't exist today. I winced when I asked for it. It was as if I said, "Give me eyes to see," while also laughing and saying, "but only just a tiny bit."

All I knew was that I wanted to continue in desire that leads to life and that I would need the guidance of the Holy Spirit to do it. The Holy Spirit is the seed. The Holy Spirit gives eyes to see and ears to hear and not of things that are temporary. We're to "fix our eyes not on what is seen, but on what is unseen, since what is seen is temporary, but what is unseen is eternal."[2]

If I wanted to see the unseen, I had to consider the prophets of old and how they saw below the surface and beyond the times. They saw how it all fit into an eternal scheme. Consider Isaiah's visions, how his desire was to see Israel trust the love of the Holy One. He warned them of the consequence of separation, how all the sacrificing and striving couldn't buy God. He saw through Israel's idolatry and how worshiping the work of their own hands would lead to their captivity. He saw a coming suffering servant Messiah and so was able to proclaim the kingdom of God-with-us Emmanuel. Consider, too, Hosea, who in spite of the idolatry and the oppression of the poor during his time, saw the opportunity for repentance. His wife played a harlot, but he loved her still. He found her and stayed with her. He lived a belovedness toward his bride, according to the prophetic vision he had of how beautiful Christ would one day make his people. He heard God say, "I will heal their apostasy; I will love them freely."[3]

The Old Testament prophets had the ability to see through to the other side of performance. Their visions were of the holy, eyes on what is unseen, instead of the flammable, shakable here and now. Their eyes were fixed according to their hope. They also had the gift to see that there is a way out, a kingdom coming, and it is the only way to be satisfied or fed or to stand before a God so holy that angels hovered at him with covered faces singing eternal greatness, so holy that mouths went void of words without the permission of coals on the tongue. They were seers, hope mongers. They saw the consequence of faith and the bald heads, ashes, separation, and destruction that would come without it.

Prophets of the new covenant seem to be much the same, only now they see through to the other side, with Messiah Jesus as the named hope today and up ahead. Today's prophets are the ones listening, the ones hanging on to the Word of God in Scripture and thereby in the Spirit, knowing that the "seen was not made out of things that are visible." "By faith we understand that the universe was created by the word of God."[4] All I knew was that his words are the makings of life.

I didn't understand practically how prophecy could change my everyday life, but I asked for the gift anyway, and I knew that the fruit of my request was good, because it was turning my heart toward his, toward love for the church. I was shocked that the more I pondered prophecy (what it is and whether or not it's even needed in our time), the more God engaged me through Scripture and the more my love kindled toward the church. Even still, I didn't know what to do about it because church was the place I felt the least at home.

Church at home and the broader church had become harder for me, especially as more and more voices poured unhindered into online spaces. Everything felt divided. But I desired to know and express Christ's love as the only love that meets in weakness, like Hosea with his wife. My desire was to see the church know Jesus from the floor up, from the root, to see us recognize our shared brokenness as the fertile place, how we are an outgrowth of life from a seed that died before it produced fruit.[5] I longed to see the church know how desired she is, to see the beautiful gift of paradox, the broken whole of us.

These desires came in intimate and quiet rest, but other than that, I just acted like a little baby lamb trying to learn legs. My knees kept getting in my own way. I desired these beautiful things while simultaneously attending church and feeling more and more misplaced. I loved the church, but I was waffling and falling into bouts of anxiety that kept me isolated from her. Sunday mornings had become like visiting a stranger, when once she had known and loved me. She had held my face and known me like a mother knows a child: the smirk, the thumb smearing dirt from the face, leaning her forehead into mine. She had been with me. She had put her hand on my back and prayed for me deep. She had made a home for me, served hot bread and good wine, but it had been a long time since I had felt that way. On Sunday mornings, I went to her, and when she opened the door, she didn't know my name, and I had a hard time recognizing her face. *Is Jesus here anymore?*

I didn't know how to find my way back home, and anxiety seemed a fair response to feeling lost. I wanted intimacy and belonging with the people of God but still had trouble reaching out because I saw in us all a deep dissatisfaction. I was chief among the dissatisfied, and reaching out to the dissatisfied church didn't make sense. The cravings for more and bigger and better left us all so wanting. Conversations were centered around maximizing growth, and this was something I didn't want to grow. Every step toward maximized growth felt like an actual shrinking, like a kingdom of the powerless, and I didn't want to be a part of that, though it's exactly what I was living out in a local context and in my writing life online. I was beginning to see church as the kingdom of the dissatisfied powerless.

If a minister of the gospel or a church wants to grow a ministry, the model has become to strive to make a great name for herself. She'll need a slogan and an exterior façade that draws the eye. I had been receiving invitations from faces pulled tight, lifted beyond the wrinkles of suffering. Everywhere seemed signs: we are beautiful here; we are rich. What of that had to do with Jesus? I wasn't sure how to see the church anymore, and I began to wonder if the prophetic vision for which I had asked was the only way I might be able to see at all, to continue toward the love offering to grow in me.

We finally found a small rental house, knowing it was temporary, and a few months later, Seth visited Ethiopia, leaving me for two winter weeks in a tiny house during an ice storm with four boys. This would feel like a desperate time for anyone, but it left a shadow over me, and I was so disappointed I had fallen into it again. When Chris Marlow invited me to come to Haiti with Help One Now—a nonprofit relief organization—in the spring of 2014, I was terrified. I knew Haiti was a most broken place, and I feared the sadness there would swallow me, all my divided pieces. Not even with Titus had I begged more during a wait. "Don't let Haiti take me," I prayed. "Don't let me fear the brokenness. Give me eyes for hope." On the flight to Haiti, I was trembling.

When we walked out of the airport in Port-au-Prince, it began, an explosion of color, the rumble of people. A Haitian pastor, Gaetan, met us to give us a ride. It was a new airport. It was city. I expected poverty in large spreads, but I didn't expect to see tin on tin as homes strung along the sides of main roads in many directions. I didn't expect the roads to look as if they had been jigsawed, how they dipped and slung to the side. Broken boards and spindles from the backs of broken chairs were nailed up into walls.

It was all broken, but there was art at every turn. Even in the thickest poverty, there was a man humming. There was the smell of spice. The faces were so beautiful it made me schoolgirl nervous. There was an easiness to the personalities there, a desire for connection that reached out in jokes and body language. I made friends in less than a day.

I went with Help One Now to do some storytelling for them, but I hadn't realized the size of the picture and how small of an organization they were. They go to Haiti as friends and supporters of the ones who are really doing the work. Something about watching Marlow with the pastors there, Pastor Gaetan and Pastor Jean Alix, felt like watching a first-century sort of brotherhood.

I hadn't realized the actual structure. Marlow is the executive director of Help One Now, but watching him with the leaders in Haiti was like witnessing a man who had come to submit to the shepherds (apostles?) of that nation. If you could hear Gaetan speak about gospel and training leaders, or if you could see Jean Alix with his arms around the orphans who have become his many sons, you would know what I mean.

We met Gaetan's wife, and the joy on her face made her one of the most beautiful women I have ever seen, this joy shining out after she had cooked a meal for thirty-one children. My eyes went straight to her feet. I had never so desired to kneel straight down and wash feet. They were not the feet of fame, and they don't belong on pedestals. These people all had the humble, desperate, persevering feet of Jesus Christ, so leave it to them to have been metaphorically washing everybody else's feet. To know them was to respect them and to want to show them honor.

Seeing the church in Haiti brought about a New Testament language in me. I saw a woman pick through garbage, gathering it with a bag, and right on the same island I saw a church so healthy that I wondered how to get every single church leader I knew to come and witness the discipleship.

We got to worship with them in a church service with families keeping watch over all the children together like family. Fathers raised their hands to sing. Young men read Scripture. It seemed that everyone had a place, the young and the women too. My mind didn't understand but three words throughout the entire thing. *Amen. Hallelujah. Hosannah.*

"Hosannah in the highest!" we all sang—they in their language, and me in mine. The woman who led worship and the young men in the band were like ones singing from a strong tower. Imagine what I saw. It was hot. The windows were open, and the wind blew the curtains straight in. Imagine them worshiping. I want you to hear us all. Imagine it, how we swayed and sang even when we didn't know the words. Imagine glory. I received something near the gift of interpretation, because never before have I understood so few words while also understanding everything. We were clothed with the same Spirit, all of us. I felt interwoven into something much greater than an island, than my little state, my own little nation.

Something happened in me, and I saw all of us there. The beautiful church. I saw with my eyes the benefits of churches coming alongside other churches, acknowledging the whole. I saw with my eyes unity. I held the fatherless, and they were the future of us all.

I saw them, and it made me long for my North American church. I longed for us to be one. I went to Haiti for a vision, to fall in love with my own people. There was no us and them. There is only us.

⚜

One morning we met at 5:00 a.m. and sardined into a car for a rickety four-hour drive way out until it wasn't city anymore. We passed where once was rain forest, the mountainside raped into sand. We passed goats and wild horses. We drove into the land of men and women bent in the middle, backs to the sky. It's the land of old men with washboard abs. All day they swing way back and around to a crack, axes to the rocks and hoes to the field. The women carry baskets on their heads with their shoulders and necks steady and regal. A few napped in wheelbarrows. The road brought us to a river, and from there a canal ran to and through Drouin. The young bathers ran naked. Women washed. Cows drank. Voodoo waved a flag nearby.

Even in the countryside, trash was everywhere, just thrown to the side for lack of infrastructure. There was still rubble everywhere from the earthquake. The poverty didn't have an end. I figured as much, but to see it was another thing. I came expecting hopelessness, but the Spirit taught me a new mantra in the midst of it, the truest thing I had known in the most contrasting setting. "He is my living hope. His joy is my strength." It was the beginning of prophecy, to see hope in the midst of pain, hope in the long wait between poverty and satisfaction.

We arrived in Drouin, carsick and hot as a Dallas tarmac, or maybe hot as a metal box on wheels full of humans at sea level in the tropics. It made us grip water bottles vertical until the last drop. I got out and stood straight in the sun. I faced a field and closed my eyes. Cows, the Haitian way of jabbing and then the rumble of men letting loose, laughter, children singing through smiley teeth. I could hear it all. A school was behind me. One class seemed to learn it all through song. I wanted to shove the sounds in a chest so I could let them out if I ever forgot. The hope I saw and heard among Jesus's people in Haiti was the kind of hope that makes the lame walk. It didn't make sense.

I turned around to a schoolhouse full of children, and when class was over, they ran to us. They ran hard and happy. It was a rush of touch, of being eye to eye. They wanted to see themselves in our phones, and so we took hundreds of photos. There were 125 children at the school because Pastor Jean Alix loved them so.

After the earthquake, after so much loss already, aid workers brought rice to the country, which turned out to be a bad case of when helping hurts. Drouin is the home of rice farmers. Free rice for all doesn't bode well for rice farmers. An entire community lost jobs and began to go hungry. Many had to feed their children every other day, if even then. Only a few short months later, cholera ran down the river and into the canal. Hundreds of thousands died in Haiti from cholera. The canal even now is Drouin's only source of water.

Drouin is full of children and so full of mamas who love their babies. Two mothers in the community told us of their love, and I knew it by heart before they even spoke it. It's what any of us feel when we see our children, know the beauty within, and believe completely that our babies are capable of everything good. These mothers spoke of their gratitude that the church was providing education, a huge meal, and jobs so that their families could move in the direction of healing after the loss of their funds for food and wellness when the world brought rice to Haiti.

I wish you could have seen them, the bright eyes and the lighter hearts of children singing and being fed. The Haitian church there in Drouin saw the babies and in them a future, the most beautiful things they'd ever seen.

Isn't that the very heart of prophecy? Isn't it to look into a place and a people, to see beyond this quaking world and into the unshakable potential? The leaders there, as a people of the unshakable kingdom, acted toward those families in the way that God sees them, as worthy, like the kingdom version of a person is the only version there is.

I looked around at us, friends I had traveled with and known for a long time and my new Haitian friends, and I saw a people in us all who weren't unacquainted with brokenness, the rubble, or the wilderness. I saw a people made for wholeness. I saw a most humble kingdom of power.[6]

There are moments in a life when everything pauses. Life runs smoothly in the definitions we've given ourselves, and then something happens like marriage or childbirth or death that screeches everything to a halt. One has to redefine herself before momentum picks back up again. To move forward is to move as someone new. This was Haiti for me, and visiting Ferrier Village, an orphanage for children trafficked along the border of the Dominican Republic, was a huge part of that.

Before we took a walk to see what was within the protective walls of the village, we sat for a home-cooked Creole breakfast. It was good and kind. Children were obediently giving us space. They were the kind of obedient that said they had a mama. One tiny one pitched a fit because she didn't want to wear her yellow dress, and we giggled. Kids are the same everywhere. Her house mother gave the look, stood her up straight, and tied that dress right back on her.

We were able to talk long about trafficking at the border. It is happening, very small ones kidnapped to be sold. The lens of a prophetic hope is the only way to see the kingdom in the midst of such devastation. Pastor Jean Alix shared his vision, and vision is a requirement in the church. Were there no hope, this book, my life, the church, and Ferrier Village would be altogether pointless.

It was hard not to weep at the conditions in which these children had been found. When those babies were rescued at the border, they were starved. Many of them had no names. Government officials asked Pastor Jean Alix to take the children they had rescued that day. They only had a jail cell to put them in. What was the church to do? We come alongside, don't we?

It didn't take long for the children with orange hair to get back their glow. Jean Alix hired good workers to build homes. There are "mothers" for each house. Now their aim is to raise these young ones up—to transition them into adulthood as functioning, contributing members of their society—but even if function is low, these children will know love.

There was one little boy with a Superman shirt whose eyes and smile pitched warm light. He slipped one quiet hand into mine as if half hoping I wouldn't notice and half hoping I would take him in my arms. He was both unassuming and willing. I squeezed his hand, and a laugh broke out his mouth. Mine too.

When it was time to leave, I wanted to shove dirt in my pockets, to run back into their Creole kitchen for a mouthful of plantains, to have the drip of ripe Haitian mango running down my arms. I ran my eyes back and forth, back and forth, to try to memorize their faces. I looked for Superman and ached in language barrier to communicate with the woman who directed the village. There was fire in me to see those children brought to healing and wholeness.

None of the good done there had a stitch to do with me, but there was a radical shift inside. The love of God swelled in me, a deep mother love, and in it I felt my own belovedness, how he must love us all.

I am a mother. I sway in a mother walk, and I have the embrace of one who is not scared of her mother body. I listen to my mother heart. When my Titus's heart was racing out of his chest, I knew something was wrong, though no one else could hear it. In it was a hole; I heard the hole in his heart, the swishing void. When his face sank in for lack of fat, I knew to take his skin to mine and feed him of my love.

There was a tiny boy in Ferrier named Lamar with a face shaped exactly like my Titus's had been. My eyes landed and my mouth whispered, *He has failure to thrive.* And then he came to me, and he dangled from my neck the rest of our time there, exactly how my Titus does. It felt nearly two hundred degrees that day, and I was made to walk for miles this way. If I had brought my boys with me, I would have carried Titus and held the hand of my middle two the entire visit, and so this is how I carried Lamar and walked with two others.

I am a mother, and Jesus has given me my mother heart, so when I had to leave after holding Lamar's face to mine, it took everything I had to walk away. If I hadn't been confident that they were being cared for by my Haitian brothers and sisters, if I didn't have a vision and a hope of the strong Haitian church, I would have imploded under concern, the lack of touch.

I ache for Lamar even now, and with the ache is joy and hope; I feel that mother love, the smile of the Spirit funneling through. The prophets always hear God whispering, "Come back to me." The prophets work out of a deep sense of belovedness. The love I experienced toward Lamar was a prophetic kind of love, my prayers holding him to God as in the hands of a mother.

We had been warned about the plane with stories of questionable pilots and failed engines, but it was the only way back to Port-au-Prince. This was the tiny blue airplane that roared like a chain saw in each ear and tipped side to side, dropping and picking back up over the mountains. It sat out in a wide, open field still lined with rubble. The engine shook the ground, and there was one among us so shaken that her entire body jumped like electrocuted nerves. We may as well had been getting on a boat in a storm. We may as well had been asked to walk on water.

Before the plane ride, we said good-bye to our translators, one of whom was called Monk because of his meek demeanor. He was a whisperer and a smiler, one always at peace. A few days before the flight, he had asked me, "Can you tell me how to keep my eyes on Jesus?" I'm not sure I answered him well, but I know my answer now.

159

Among the church in Haiti, I witnessed a people who saw the unseen, and I, too, received the gift. I saw Jesus in the church there. Keeping my eyes on him in my everyday life has come to mean that I recognize the fruit of the Spirit in others while simultaneously acknowledging him as my hope up ahead, the one sitting at the right hand of the Father. I see through to the other side of the visible, through to the unseen, the kingdom of God and how we fit into this kingdom. I recognize Jesus because I know him, and keeping my eyes on him means to see through this world to him, how holy potential hides in us all.

His kingdom is everywhere for those who have the eyes to see, like how Jean Alix saw the babies not as fatherless orphans but as beloved sons.

The night before that roarous flight back to Port-au-Prince, we had a Caribbean dinner at a long table, and Monk told me that he saw Jesus in me too. I put my forehead to the table so he couldn't see me cry.

There's no way to know what Monk had endured, because he kept a smile, but I asked him, "What is the thing you want most for your life?" His response still has me reeling. He said, "I want for nothing, and I want for everything." He wanted better for Haiti. He wanted healing in relationships, but he explained that there wasn't a thing he didn't have in Christ. He walked a life of contentment on the tension between already but not yet. He looked like Jesus.

I left that conversation, and I knew exactly what I wanted for the rest of my life—for nothing and for everything. I thought, how unjealous I am of anyone on this planet. All I ever want for myself is the kingdom version of me, the exact thing he is making me. All I ever want to be said of my sons is that to be with them is to be near Jesus.

There's a certain amount of surrender and release that has to happen in Haitian air. Riding in that plane was proof of an older version of myself falling off. It was the feeling of being ready to meet my Maker, of being exactly where I was supposed to be, with my heart singing, "Kingdom come."

Weeks later, I reached in my pocket and pulled out a handful of Haitian sand. Along the sea-urchin, reef-lined coast, three of us had wanted to be as naked as newborns in the waters, but instead I had walked into the ocean with my pants on. Weeks later in my own Arkansas home, I pulled out a handful of Haiti. When I was there, I told the people in the car with me that I felt like a chemical had washed over my brain. It was the quantum physics of an invisible thing being realized, what some call a miracle. I experienced this one time before. It was the day I first believed, the day I forgot to smoke cigarettes and no longer craved any sort of substance.

Before I left for Haiti, I asked Isaac what he knew of Haiti, and he really knew nothing. I mentioned the earthquake, and he immediately responded with, "Why would God ever do something like that?" I said, "Baby, I don't think anybody can know why that happened, but I do know that the earth was made to quake. Tectonic plates were made to move along the molten surface. This is how mountains and islands were made in the first place." The earth was made to quake. Swallow that one.

And then I read of the unshakable kingdom,[7] and when I read it, a vision formed in me.

When I left for Haiti, I felt the shaking. I was quaking way down inside, fear and trembling. This whole world is beautiful, and it is shaking. It is in ruins, and yet, sunshine beams through drips of rain strung like rainbow beads on a spider's web. Great things are being revealed, and great things are falling away. When I left home, I feared that witnessing such poverty would strip me of every last ounce of joy, but instead I witnessed the intended version of myself by way of recognizing the beautiful church. I felt a shift in my own definition.

I am not afraid to go to God anymore like Israel was long ago at Mount Sinai, like when Moses trembled in the presence of the blazing light of God. Mount Sinai was the meeting place for the reception of the law, and it was a mountain born as all mountains were, from the quaking, from a bursting upward rub of hot ground.

Haiti can tell you that things are still shaking like this today. The world is still pushing up, quaking, and burning down. We're always talking about the kingdoms shaking down around us, about this culture, the wars, and the tired church machine, how in this world we will have trouble.

But when we go to God now, when we take heart that Jesus has overcome the shakable world, we no longer go to his presence at Mount Sinai, where God shined so untouchably holy that Moses had to cover his face, and an idiot ass would die if it leaned against the mountain where God stood.

Now is a new thing. Now the Spirit is with us, and we are journeying to Mount Zion, where we will not shake but rather be invited to feast with the living God. We will be welcomed into the kind of awe that opens eyes to see wing on wing on wing, a myriad of angels. We of every land will come to an assembly, a church beautiful with her veil pulled way back, shining. She won't be covered up like Moses. She'll be out in the open with unshakable God. She will finally be home.

Hope of the Exiled

After Haiti, I couldn't seem to shift back into any regular mode of living, and thank goodness for that. If the poverty and then the contrasting and active love of Christ through the Haitian church hadn't been enough, then the conversation I had on my last day there with local leader St. Cyr itself would have permanently damaged the way I understood church and my role in it. In other words, St. Cyr messed with my identity without even meaning to.

A few of us had decided to stay an extra day in Port-au-Prince to spend time with friends who live there, and it landed me across the lunch table from St. Cyr. I had just walked with him and his son through a new church building and school, and while we were in that beautiful building, he told me that money is a little thing for God. The building was new and built right where the church started, right where the tent city sprung up after the earthquake. St. Cyr worshiped Jesus every night in the center of that tent city in the days following the quake, and as he and his friends worshiped, hope swelled and the church grew. The church grew among a people who were literally starving, people who had lost everything, *and I mean everything*.

Four years after this great shaking of Haiti, we were able to sit down in a restaurant that was much like a Haitian Hooters. The girls wore tank tops tucked into their shorts. It was a clean, nice place, and the framed posters on the wall were of women and hot peppers or women in chains. The men had a restroom inside, and the women had to go out. St. Cyr and his son weren't afraid of the world at all, not the trash, not the sexuality, not the homeless starved. There was no fear. We sat in Hooters in the tension between slavery and freedom, and I caught a glimpse of the kingdom of God.

Sitting across from St. Cyr, I asked him three questions, and then he preached to me in the kind of booming voice that can only come from a giant. He preached for a solid forty-five minutes.

My first question was, "How did you come to be such a leader?" He then went the long way about telling me that he is not a leader. "No one but Jesus leads,"[1] he said, and then he described how he is merely a servant. He loves to care for the caregivers, and he serves care to caregivers until they become better caregivers. In other words, this is how he makes leaders.

He told me the story of his upbringing and all his opportunities to stay in the States to make money. His desire, though, was for Haiti. This is when I asked him the question, "Do you feel like you chose to be poor?"

Once it came out of my mouth, I realized my perspective was off. He put his hands to the table and leaned his body back. "Let me explain something to you," he said. That's when I knew I'd better settle in to my chair.

He explained to me the riches of our faith. It was profound. "If God lives in you by the indwelling of the Holy Spirit, and you're not distracted or pacified by your own cravings and desires, then your life is so full of fruit, a deep satisfaction, that you would never call that *poor*. This is what it means to be poor in spirit, and the poor in spirit are the very ones who inherit the kingdom of heaven."[2] He explained further, told me how the faith of a poor spirit, one that isn't distracted by its own desires, acts itself out in willingness to work and give, because this person is satisfied in the richness of God. A believer knows where her help comes from.

He described how satisfied individuals comprise a satisfied church who doesn't receive the kingdom of heaven only when this life is over but also as we ask that the kingdom come on this earth as it is in heaven.

Building on his comments on the satisfied church, I asked him, "Did you know that people are leaving the American church in droves?" and this is when I thought my brain would explode.

"American culture never allows you to be satisfied," he said. "When you want something, you go after it and get it, and as soon as you do, you want for something else, maybe a thousand more things. American culture will never have enough. It stands to reason that the church would follow suit."

St. Cyr said that as long as people make a god of relevancy and of gain, they will never be satisfied with the church. The leaders and church structures will never be able to offer what it is people *feel* like they need. If Jesus can't be packaged and sold to the liking of the congregants, a desire-driven, unsatisfied people will leave.

It was as if he had taken my idea of kingdom and put it in one of those shakers behind the bar. He shook me and my ideas. Oh, how shakable was my idea of church, but we are of an unshakable kingdom. So where is the discrepancy?

I was not on the island of Patmos to receive such a revelation as John's, but I was on an island, and I did receive a vision. I saw the American church, and it was a marketplace. It was in the slavery of debt, creating more product to keep itself afloat. I saw the church, and it had syncretized Jesus with consumerism, a new religion. I saw us, and we were self-proclaimed and congratulated leaders on a platform. We were not exiles like the beautiful prophet Daniel, who even under Babylonian captivity lived as a member of the kingdom of God with wisdom, courage, and satisfaction. We were fat and unsatisfied like kingdom-building Babylon. And when we were thrown in with lions, we became the lions. We were the consumers eating each other alive, consuming each other as products until we were nearly gone, until we saw ourselves as exiles again.

Consider what it means to be in exile, to be a servant embodied by God in a shakable and unsatisfied land. Consider that the kingdom of God is a kingdom of healing and reconciliation, of full satisfaction for the individual, the church, the field, the forest, nations, and the whole earth. Isn't that what we say we believe? We homeless ones will find our home, though it may take a walk through the wilderness of unmet desire to get there. It may take exposing the hollowness of our own desire to know the satisfaction of the wild love of God.

And if we are exiles together, then shouldn't we call ourselves the church, global and unshakable? Shouldn't we figure out the ways we've syncretized our shakable desires with our faith, with the power structures of this world, and dismantle the syncretization? Should we reassemble on the unshakable Mount Zion?

Sometimes we become so close to something that we can't see what it is anymore. Once I got back home to Arkansas, I had to spend some time observing my life, to see what it is I really wanted. I had to look in the mirror and listen to what came out of my heart.

In my reflection, I remembered the days before Haiti, how I thought my eyes weren't as bright as they used to be. I considered how I touched the age spot on my left cheek, darker now. I remembered wanting a visit to Sephora for some magical cream. I had made a plan for my body. I wanted a plan for anything at all. I stood on the scales and let that decide hope. I wanted for beauty. Beauty is power. I would never have said this out loud, but I acted it out in so many ways. I wanted a magazine instructing me how to be better at wanting.

In the mirror, I said, "Not enough."

In the pantry, I said, "Not enough."

I stood back and listened to desire. I took note of every single time I heard it, and it was all the time: "Not enough."

I remembered standing at the closet, grabbing the same shirt I always do but wanting for more—hail to the style. I imagined us at our next gathering. *What will my clothes say about me? Who am I?*

I once hid the shoes I bought so Seth wouldn't know. I let money carry the weight of guilt. I watched how my desire for beauty overpowered my guilt. Or I thought it would. I stood back for days and watched my efforts to heal myself with wanting.

In the days following Haiti, I didn't talk about our consumer-driven culture, but I did observe the habits of my own thoughts. I walked the dog and thought about our yard, wanted the flowerbeds, and let the desire for a garden consume me. I wanted to be home. I wanted land, to grow something good.

I unloaded the dishwasher and wanted dishes that matched. I wanted to get more of the good coffee and a better coffeemaker. I always wanted sugar. I wanted to taste sweet in my mouth all day long. I wanted to be healed.

I wrote a blog post and wanted to be understood. I checked back in ten minutes. Did anyone care? Is my platform growing? How can I make my platform grow so I can know that my words matter? I wanted the gift of powerful words. I wanted power, wanted to have something to offer, to be known. How much do you want to be known? How often, in the church, are we thinking about being known?

What consumes us? If out of the heart the mouth speaks,[3] what do we talk about? My life is built on nothing less than what I buy and how I dress.

When I came home from Haiti, I spent a few days to really know what it is that I want. Every wandering of my mind was a want, and every want led to another want. There's nothing wrong with the wanting, right? God made the beauty. He made the flowers, our voices. But spend a day and realize what's woven into the wanting. Realize the power. Realize the self-soothing and the scheming. I realized how even when I propped my feet, my mind was consumed.

As I woke up to all the wanting, I saw an unsatisfied people, a lonely people. I saw my own lonely heart, how I wanted for friends. I wanted to go to church and have them make it better. I looked inside the church bulletin. What do they have for sale? What will their women's ministry offer me? Do I buy it? Is this our economy?

Seth had to stop drinking alcohol, had come face-to-face with his addiction, but I came to believe that many in our church culture are addicted. The North American church is caught in the undercurrent of consumption, and it has become our own slavery, our not-enoughness, where upstanding ministers have to package faith and sell it at a good price so they can keep food on their own tables. It's in the letters our missionaries send home so we'll keep sending checks, when so often many of them don't even know what they believe anymore. Do we know how they're really doing? Or is this a buying and selling of the Good News? Is this why we use so many clichés and tie so many beautiful bows on suffering? Using the tidy answers and outlines is often the way we discount those in pain. We don't have to listen when we already know the answers, and oftentimes the ones giving these packaged answers and sermons are the ones suffering the most. The fruit of this kind of addiction, addiction to desire and prosperity, is hopelessness.

I looked around and saw paralysis. I had been watching dear ones walk away from the church, so many of us isolating ourselves. Many leave, wanting something that sustains, and what they had been calling the church is not what sustains. In fact, the church was never meant to be the sustainer.

Once I woke to my own thoughts and how they join the chorus of this world to say, "Not enough," I realized how numb I had been, how I had used the wanting of desire to sedate myself from feeling, from hearing my God. I had been plugged into the anesthesia.

Drip . . . "Your shopping cart is ready and waiting."

Drip . . . "Be more relevant to fulfill your rock-star potential."

Drip . . . "A large reach means greater impact. Set your podium higher."

Drip . . . "Work more mind-numbing hours and then you'll have enough."

When I woke to my own paralysis, how plugged in to the sickness I had been, I reached over and ripped that IV right out. It was like stepping out of an old body, pulling cords out of the wall, pulling hangers out of the closet. It was personal. It was a lot of unsubscribing. Every no I said was a clearer perspective of how the kingdom of this world had controlled me. I had been a servant of buying and selling. How could I hope for health in the church if I didn't actively address my own syncretized faith?

But as it turned out, it wasn't all as easy as ripping out an IV or pulling hangers out of the closet. I pulled at the cords and the roots, and there wasn't an end to them. The wanting was an endless echo, and I was the canyon. So even here, in this desire to be satisfied with God, I did what I do when I can't control things. I freaked out.

My mind habit is to roll straight into anxiety, but I knew the truth. By this point, I knew the broken way, and I felt hopeless in it, so hopeless that I walked up to my friend Angela behind the coffee bar and reached across to her. She followed me to my seat and prayed as I confessed how I feared my inability.

I confessed how unsatisfied I had been and how God had not been enough for me, and this became the turning point, the invisible part of transformation that no one can skip—confession and repentance. Even if I had sold everything I owned to give to the poor, I wouldn't have been free without confession and repentance, and aren't those some archaic words? Change wasn't going to happen for me without this invisible part that involved a knowing, trust, and rest so secure that I was able to face my own empty desires.

To the eye, repentance is not as sexy as a garage sale for orphans. Repentance involves sorrow, and in the sorrow, I had to realize the difference between grief and guilt.

There was a terrible ache when my eyes opened to how weak I was even after such a beautiful experience in Haiti, how all my mind habits—the constant desires for community, intimacy, healthy babies, and wealth—were a hunting for satisfaction outside of the Spirit of God. Guilt and shame always say that there is no hope, but the sorrow that comes with repentance[4] told me that hope is all I have.

I saw a pattern, how I fear shame and hopelessness, and so I run from grief and sadness. I confuse grief and sadness with shame and hopelessness, when really it's necessary that I sit in the grief. The sadness is hard but important along a journey of hope. When I bypass repentance's sorrow, the sadness turns to despair.

Repentance is a sorrow toward one's own sin, a recognized need, and a change of mind. Repentance is the turning point, a place of very active transformation and also a place of release. Repentance always has a directive, a place to go. Repentance is the opposite of being stuck. When I exposed my thoughts to my friend and my God, I was not stuck pulling forever at the roots.

In repentance, I went to God with my sadness, and I put my eyes back on his love instead of exhausting myself by clawing at the cords that entangled me. Repentance was the turning point, not the clawing. Repentance is not living in heaped-up shame because I would like a new pair of earrings. It isn't about earrings at all, in fact. It isn't about how much I give away or how much I'm willing to suffer. Rather, repentance is the grieving of something lost or something that feels wasted; it's the recognition that you chased other desires when you could have had God—your satisfaction—all along.

There is sorrow that comes in repentance, but it's a comforting kind of sorrow that brings rest and release. Repentance is not in the fight. The kingdom of God is not the battle against flesh and blood,[5] and sugar, and clothes, and statistics, and insurance companies, and drug lords. It is against the powers pulling at our hearts, and only the indwelling Spirit of God gives strength to fight them.

"Being asked by the Pharisees when the kingdom of God would come, he answered them, 'The kingdom of God is not coming in ways that can be observed, nor will they say, "Look, here it is!" or "There!" for behold, the kingdom of God is in the midst of you.'"[6] Yes, there is an indwelling kingdom, and transformation is not as easy or as hard as cleaning out closets or eating a cleaner diet or giving a good sermon. It's not as easy or as hard as staying in your old country church or starting a new church. In fact, it's not as easy as *doing anything*. "For the kingdom of God is not a matter of eating and drinking but of righteousness and peace and joy in the Holy Spirit."[7]

After repentance, obedience is the moving forward into righteousness, peace, and joy. This is what propels the kingdom of God. It is both restful and active. Repentance opens the eyes to this kind of active kingdom.

Say, for example, you wouldn't normally consider walking for forty days through the desert. I woke up to my wanting, in the healing kind of sorrow, and I found myself unafraid to walk through my own desert with the devil of my desire.[8] I had been released from that old syncretized faith, and at first I felt starved, like I hadn't eaten for days. I had peeled back that surface-level wanting, and my eyes opened. I saw the options before me with the perspective of one standing on the edge of a mountain.

I looked down at the kingdom of my desires and saw the palaces and positions. What I really mean is this: I imagined all my glory. Imagine with me: I am the one who sells the most books. Imagine that everyone loves me. Imagine that my children never screw up, that I make so much money, gain influence, and live in the most eco-friendly house. Imagine with me that my church becomes the biggest in town and that I'm associated with every world changer. Imagine all the wanting, all the friends. Would that glory sustain me?

I asked myself, do I want my kingdom here in the big, loud, visible now, or do I want the kingdom of heaven, the kingdom of the small, the kingdom for the broken, the kingdom of the invisible? Only one is satisfactory. Only one King can tie the church back together. Only one is the healer of my mind, my body, and my soul.

It was the Holy Spirit who led Jesus into the wilderness, and I believe we face the same temptations that he did in the wilderness. We should all hope to have our exile experience and find ourselves satisfied in barren lands. What I saw in Haiti, in that rubble, was the fruit of the Spirit, the invisible traits of the personality of Christ, multiplying out of barrenness. These are the traits that will change the church and the world, and these are in the Spirit alone.

In the desert, the tempting offer is always power, kingdom, and glory. The tempting offer is to add to material. But the invitation from Jesus to the poor in spirit, to those who find their desires fulfilled by his kingdom, is better:

> Come, everyone who thirsts,
>   come to the waters;
> and he who has no money,
>   come, buy and eat!
> Come, buy wine and milk
>   without money and without price.

Why do you spend your money for that which is not
    bread,
    and your labor for that which does not satisfy?
Listen diligently to me, and eat what is good,
    and delight yourselves in rich food.
Incline your ear, and come to me;
    hear, that your soul may live.[9]

Whole
in Sick Places

For our fifteen-year anniversary, Seth and I traveled to Tuscany with a small group of writers for a spiritual retreat that made space for inspiration by art, agriculture, history, and landscape. We couldn't think of a better way to celebrate the years we had learned to love each other or a better way to bless the years to come. We had no idea how right we were. By the time we left Italy, we had tasted metaphors on our tongues, what a juxtaposition between Italy and Haiti.

We had taken the drive from Florence into the heart of Tuscany, where tall, skinny cypress trees pointed up like arrows. "Remember heaven," they said. I rode in the van with half strangers and listened to Seth gab on and on. I am usually the gabby one. I'm usually honed in to the stories around me, but I was busy looking at ancient walls that were still in use. I was busy with red begonias and terra-cotta and how not a single scrap of trash had landed on the roadside. Children ran about yards, and the elderly sat at open windows smiling, toothless and respected.

As we drove in, I sensed a kind of order to the land and the people that I had only read about in books. It was a land that upheld its beauty like an honor. It was a land that worked but didn't strive. We heard about the winters there, yes, how hard they were, but everyone we met seemed fully aware of their blessedness. Gratitude edged the walkways. The woman in her handmade housedress swept with her broom of twigs like she might be a song away from dancing in the street.

As we unloaded our bags from the van, it was as if I opened my mouth and someone poured a spoon of sugar on my tongue. Jasmine climbed up arched doorways, and lavender grew waist high in such bunches that it doused us in relaxed air. The gate, floors, roadways, and walls of the villa were from the 1200s, and it seemed repair had been done brick by brick, in constant care and attention.

The ten in our group cried as we entered our house that would be our residence for the week. I write it like it was a dramatic thing because it was just that beautiful. The backyard bounced with honeybees and also with hummingbirds so tiny I thought they were bees too. Starlings darted through the air drawing pictures across the great, wide sky over miles and miles of olive groves and vineyards. Everything thrived and hummed. It was as if the veil between here and glory was so thin that if you squinted your eyes just right, you thought it might be possible to see the spirit world forget to be invisible for a minute.

Old men drove their bicycles up the hill to sit on the quiet bench and watch the land turn into soft fabric with shifting sunlight. We watched and learned how to listen with them. *Sh . . . life is humming.* There is room for pondering. Words can be bookended with quiet. All is contentment. Tuscany taught us the order of such things.

The tiny villa was on a hill, like a lookout to a thousand other hills. On one side of our hill was a restaurant, where we watched the sun go down in a color only found otherwise in coral reefs.

The first table we shared as a group was not in a fancy room but in that little restaurant, where our waitress had spindly hair in every direction and wore an apron. Her brother was the cook. It seems the place had been open for only a short time, because they were just as grateful to have us there as we were to be smelling such a scene: garlic and tomatoes and hand-rolled pici, the wine, the cheese, and the salami. It was as if we never believed what we had heard, as if our overconnected world hadn't ever given us any hints. It was all more than we could possibly have expected.

Even in such a sensory explosion of color, sound, and smell, it was the table experience that overwhelmed the most. Our table was long, and our faces hurt from laughing. My teeth were dry from smiling. The waitress brought platters that were three feet wide, and every time we would moan in disbelief that there was more to eat. We rolled our eyes and used two hands to pass the plate, men to women, women to men, brand-new friends passing the plate like a rite into siblinghood, a shared blessedness.

From table to table, we were revealed this way, into brothers and sisters. Our laughter became more and more boisterous, and our tears sat closer to the surface. We were each becoming something bare.

As we made our little drives through Tuscany, we continued to see joy again and again in the work, and this, too, unveiled us, like an answer to a riddle we didn't know we heard. Who knows what any of those fine folks knew of Jesus, but I saw kingdom in the metaphors, especially in the metaphor of place and of enjoying good work. The farmers we met loved their position in life. They loved the dirt in nails and their calling to feed others real food. They told stories of organic food like the gospel, and it showed me passion. The owner of the home where we stayed spoke of how much she loved to organize and create authentic Tuscan experiences for others. I saw the joy of doing what one loves.

We listened to Luciano tell us of his olive grove, how hundreds of years grew his trees to great widths, how inside the trees is always a dying trunk, how they'll cut out the center, the death, and let one tree become three separate trees, and then how the root system is so connected that each tree is dependent on the others. His holy trinity of trees connected to other trinities of trees—these were his tender fruits.

The grapes in his palms were his beloved daughters. His blue eyes were lakes atop fire red cheeks. That devilish smile—how he could make a woman laugh. Luciano was the happiest man, and his son had come to love the fruit too. This was his greatest joy, the passing down.

In the house where we stayed, women came to launder our dirty clothes, and when they folded them clean, they made each stack precisely the size of an elegant basket and tied the stacks with a bow. In each bow were fresh flowers. They loved the special touch. They loved their work. I saw this love of work everywhere, how the old man etched at leather and the young man proudly scooped his father's gelato. People who love their work, who are content in their craft, are people who can understand a deeper metaphor about having a place to belong.

Maybe the slices of life we witnessed were extraordinary and rare, but I know what I saw. The way each person seemed to take joy in her work and giftings was the way she fit into her community and moved it toward wholeness. The workers knew the burden of work, but they also knew joy, because they used their gifts to do what they loved. The women tying roses to my folded sweater and socks were women who felt life in the giving.

But it didn't stop there. The individual isn't the end of such gifts. The healing and wholeness of one brings healing and wholeness of the community. This was another peek into my own God desire, into the economy of a healthy church, operating from contentedness in the kingdom. I had a vision of the church while in Tuscany, but maybe it wasn't about church anymore. Maybe all along we were supposed to seek first the kingdom,[1] the actual whole of us in an unshakable place.

The word *kingdom* isn't one we use much, except to pray, "Thy kingdom come"[2] and "For thine is the kingdom, and the power, and the glory."[3] But I'm not sure I have ever really known what God asked of me when he required that I seek first his kingdom and his righteousness, or what I asked of him when I prayed for his kingdom to come on earth as it is in heaven.

Is it God on the throne inside the castle and my working in the fields to be seen by him so that he'll have favor on me? After Italy, I'm positive that it is not.

When we seek the kingdom, I believe we're seeking a proper order and placement of things. I believe we're seeking a table and we're doing work that gives life. I believe we walk in glory, and it becomes our joy to turn our hearts in the direction of the King, who works not from the castle and not beside but from within. The King is our friend. The King no longer calls us servants.[4] We aren't working in the field away from him. We work in communion. We share in the suffering of his labor, yes, but we share in his joy too.

When we each left Tuscany, we had been changed in different ways. I left able to do something I had never been able to do in my life. I was able to say the thing I desired. I was able to have a want and weigh it in my heart. Is this seed from the Father of lights? What will this seed become?

When I left Tuscany, I wanted to root down and live the metaphors of land, of dependence on rain and shine. I wanted to walk with my sons in a garden. I wanted to teach them about place, about humility, about knowing where we are in honesty, a speck of blue dust floating in the corner of a swirling galaxy. I wanted to teach them of space, of making room for the voice of God and serving those around them in joy. I wanted to teach them of time and gravity, how short and heavy, how our bodies don't perceive eternity without an eye for invisible things.

I desired to know a kingdom economy, a working together that sees beyond the outlines and formulas, one that envisions others as a fingertip, an eye, a heel, the strong thigh of the body of Christ. I desired to watch the inner workings of seeds and to pull up thorns, to throw out the cares of this world like something that strangles my own babies. I desired for revolution in the church, the un-American way, the holy, holy, holy of the kingdom come. I desired to see a kingdom mind-set, a corporate hallelujah, confession, and pang of heart. I desired to have all desire wrapped up in Jesus.

I desired a rest so full, a Sunday rest, a Sabbath of honey, for the weary bones to reassemble. I desired to wake up Monday mornings and see the fit of kingdom, to enter into the rhythm of seasons, to understand the time.

What do I want? Desire always points to the kingdom I serve.

So I cannot live without the church, because she and I are one. The years I spent in isolation from her divided my heart against the kingdom of God, so of course my desires were confused, and I had no fit. "Whoever isolates himself seeks his own desire; he breaks out against all sound judgment."[5]

There is hardly healing of the self outside the church because the Spirit always moves us forward into living as our whole selves, as friends who love what he loves, and he loves us. He makes us whole as individuals, and then we are propelled forward with desire to be healing agents of his kingdom. It is about the whole of us, global.

This economy even works in my home. My son Jude and I are either embracing or clashing at all times because we are so much alike, and when I am living my gifts of encouragement and helping Scripture come alive for young ears, he tends to live more into his gifts as well. I tell him what I read in Scripture that morning, and I even share how some of it doesn't make sense to me, and he weaves the story I tell him like a visionary, a lover of justice, and a spreader of joy. Even though my children and my husband know more than anyone how I have struggled, when one of us seeks the kingdom, our home is a domino effect of healing.

Depression and anxiety may be avenues of surrender that I have to walk until I die. Yet I am still lacking in nothing. I was made for joy. When I laugh, it is a loud invitation. God gave me teeth big enough to blind you with a glare when I smile. When I am living out my gifts and walking in the fruit of the Spirit, I know good and well my place. My life is *poema*, and it lacks no tension. I have always been weak, but it is his joy that makes me strong,[6] that gives me a fit among his people.

I am lacking in nothing, and that does not mean I have had no weakness. It only means that his "steadfast love is before my eyes."[7] Life flows in me like a paint stroke at creation when my eyes are open to how solidly he loves. He loved me first.[8] This is the entire thing. This is the essence, the meat, and the foundation of his kingdom. His love is a force that turns me fearless and giving, even in the midst of rubble.

Anxiety and depression dry the bones. His love is blood reaching every part. His love awakens the dying parts, knits me back together, mind, body, and soul. I am awake to my love, first love who held me on a linoleum floor, first love who became my kin, a shared bloodline kind of kin. I fold my arms around my husband, because I live out my healing in the metaphor. My marriage is the most intimate place where I learn that isolation is a work against the healing of the whole.

I have cut myself off from my husband and my God in the past, because I have lived with my eyes on my body, on the beautiful metaphors of making love and children and art. I have shopped as if fashion could give me a name. I have been so hungry for confections. I have stirred up my attentions in every way possible for making a safe place: friendships and land with a garden and a pretty house. I have worshiped the metaphors that were all given to speak of Jesus, and so of course they have been twisted into things so desirous that they acted as consuming fires in longing for his place. They became the idols that feed on envy. They became insatiable jealous beasts, when God says that he is the jealous one, jealous enough to die. Yet he is life. Yet he is steadfast love. He met me on the floor, and he meets me still.

I have yet to see a single metaphor be completely satisfying unto itself. The meal can be a soul's idea of the perfect metaphor, but the stomach is empty again before day's end. We need food to make us strong, and even then we consume foods that work against the body; and, when it comes to the soul, we forget the spiritual food altogether. The kingdom of this world is broken (what we can see with our eyes, carry on platters, decide in courtrooms, and gain by collecting in houses and bank accounts), and yet we spend entire lives working within the broken structure to find our strength. We live as if the metaphor will save us, when the metaphors were only ever made to point us to God.

Watch the United States of America. Watch us call ourselves strong and free until we've crumbled under the weight of what we've consumed and are consuming. We are overweight and in debt. We want our nation to stand for freedom, and our perching eagle says we do. The eagle is a metaphor and my very favorite metaphor for freedom. We want to own the strength it represents by having a strong economy and by being a leader in diplomacy and security, but this is not lasting strength. This is not the strength that carries the people of God. He says that "those who hope in the Lord will renew their strength. They will soar on wings like eagles; they will run and not grow weary, they will walk and not grow faint."[9] What makes us strong? Strength always comes from hope. A sick nation is not a good hope.

We are weak ones, but this is not bad news. Isn't brokenness the fertile ground for the seed of hope, the low place where Jesus meets us? We are weak, and we were made for hope, and until we find our true hope, there is no strength. The metaphors, no matter how complete they may seem, cannot be my hope. They will not make me strong, not my marriage and not my children. The metaphors of this life often prove brokenness, and hope is what pulls the tension, what moves us in love through the brokenness toward the healing. God's love is before my eyes, and it is staid. It is my hope. I keep my eyes on him. If I do not see his love, it is my eyes that have moved.

If you were to ask me what I understand about the purpose of church and the Sunday service, I would say it is to meet together to remember and ingest our shared brokenness in Christ, to remember the pouring out. We meet for communion. We meet like hungry kids at a table. We meet to confess that all our desires are filled in the life of Christ, broken and resurrected for us.

But church is not only Sunday morning; the kingdom is not for a mere day of the week. We know this with our brains. Church is not the sign out front or the people on our elder boards. Church is not made up of followers of Pastor so-and-so or active through successful committee meetings. You are church, you together with all who believe on this living rock.

It is so beautifully simple. We are a priesthood.[10] Your whole self (body, mind, and soul) is a temple, and Holy Spirit God indwells you.[11] He is a complete and whole God within you. He is every fruit and every gift, every single thing you need for life and godliness.[12] Life is an exciting and mysterious unveiling of his goodness within us. He is the satisfaction of all our desires.

So often we aren't open to such goodness because we're distracted. We're distracted as consumers of church. We want the exact satisfactions that tempted Jesus on his walk in the wilderness, but he resisted the kingdoms of the world and showed us a life that is completely satisfied in his Father. If we resist chasing every wind of desire, we get to walk the same relationship with the same Father as Jesus. We are church, and the gospel makes us so. There is no believing and leaving church. We are the church, satisfied in God alone.

I do not care if you're in a bar, a ditch, a hospital bed, or behind a podium on stage. I don't care if you were born mute or blind or with Down syndrome. I don't care if you're rolling in cash or looking on the sidewalk for change. Are you the man who changes light bulbs or picks up trash in the stadium? Are you the one who prays exquisite prayers? It does not matter where you are, who you are, or how educated you are. In Christ, you are the church.

Are you a woman allowed no role other than to keep nursery? That does not bind you. Nothing can bind you. There is no physical, spiritual, or scientific law against what Jesus calls fruit. If we are in him, and satisfied by him, then we bear it, and we will be known by these invisible qualities and the actions born thereof. These are what it means to be complete in Christ.[13]

These are the building blocks of a revolution from the kingdom of this world to the kingdom of God: "love, joy, peace, patience, kindness, goodness, faithfulness, gentleness, self-control; against such things there is no law."[14] There is not a soul on this planet who wouldn't be drawn in and changed by such good and free fruit. There's not a church that wouldn't be brought to health. There's not a nation that wouldn't begin to bend toward the image of Jesus.

Think of the man of peace, how he heaped coals of kindness. Think of his goodness, how he multiplied the little, his faithfulness, his love that stayed through rooster crows. He bucked social trends to heal, to bring completeness. He healed a crippled woman on the Sabbath. He told her to get up and walk.[15] That is the very Spirit who makes us. Do we believe him? Do we believe that the Spirit's embodying brings completeness? Do we know that completeness isn't in an organization, conference, or program that serves up "church" to be consumed like a business serves up a product? We are branches meant to live (abide) only in our Jesus, the social-rule breaker, our Jesus, the water walker and law fulfiller. He fulfills every jot and tittle, every reason for law by being love, joy, peace, patience, kindness, goodness, faithfulness, gentleness, and self-control. He himself is love.

There's not a place he doesn't belong. He fills every space. Revolution doesn't start in pulpits or with elder boards, though support from those places would sure be nice. The kind of revolution needed in the North American church and in the world is going to start in the lowest places. It starts in the manger. It starts on bathroom floors. It starts in the lonely and in those crushed by shame. It starts in those in the rubble, in the needy poor in spirit.

Those who see the lack of satisfaction in the church feel like they're dying for it. Some of us give up because all we see is the brokenness, but it's a blind and hurt soul who refuses to be loved right where she is. Hope propels us. Even in the midst of corruption, Jesus has given us a Spirit, not of fear but of power, of love, and of a sound mind.[16] Jesus has given us the Spirit of completeness.

If our churches are sick, that's perfect, because he came for the sick.[17] Yes, the church is full of those who feel incredibly righteous, but we shouldn't start there and get distracted by the ones claiming that nothing ails them. The Holy Spirit within us is a despiser of shame, so start there instead. Jesus came to bring the kingdom to the poor in spirit.[18] Let's go to the poor in spirit, to the suffering; let's go, despising their shame. Go to the whore. Go to the one who stole from the plate. Go to the ones who know they will never add up. Go like he came to us. Go to the one who thinks he'll never know love. Go like the Great Commission is the truth of the matter. Go to the lonely. Go to the pothead kid and the woman who has starved herself for years. Revolution starts low, with the outsiders, even with the despised ones (Samaritans), women and cripples and whores and thieves and children. Go to the ones with special needs.

Are we not all needy? If we want to see gospel happen in our churches, we must see from a thousand miles above the little building, which is to say, we need to see the small. We need to see the things thrown to the side. Who is on the floor, without a place?

So what do we do with leaders who are living contrary to our Jesus? What do we do with those who fill our desires with a twisted gospel? For such a time as this, we love them. We speak words of blessing. We clean their toilets. We wash their feet. If we want the church to be like Jesus, then we must be like Jesus. If we want the church to look like Jesus, to show how all desires are fulfilled in him alone, then we must be ministers of the gospel right where we are.

Instead of leaving the church, we show up and go underground. We are undercover practitioners of discernment, those who sniff out pain. We worship him everywhere, carry him with us, aware of our community's desires, their wants for hope. We are not distracted by the surface things, the buying and selling, the committee meetings. Those are not our business. Our business is to seek out those who are poor in spirit, the lonely, and the ones dying of shame. Our business is to love our enemies and to forgive those who persecute us. Our business is to model how all desires are summed up in Christ.

The models of buy and sell and the models of pedestaled believers being rock-starred into leadership can be a tricky way to follow. Without bad intention, these leaders can become the models of not-enoughness. Jesus warns us to be weary of such models. Accidental kingdoms are popping up everywhere. Know that when you meet someone working hard to be outwardly beautiful and fit for consumption, inside they may be wasting away. Bookmark them with love, because if they burn out, if they become the lowly and see their misplaced desires, they'll need arms to hold them and dinner tables where brothers and sisters pass the plate.

We've all been the empty ones. The real leader is the servant to all. The leader is the one who washes feet, the one who makes herself equal to the least person in the room. You say you want a revolution? Then be like the good revolutionary. Work from right desire fulfilled; work from an intimate abiding in a love that propels.

Keep watch. Watch Jesus start with the hungry. Be hungry. Take the bread and give thanks like a child. Serve the bread and give thanks for that too. Be the child with your brothers and your sisters. Live the gospel and be a healing agent in your local church by being intimately aware of the Spirit within you. Don't you dare run from pain, from the poor in spirit. Through the poor in spirit, through us, may the kingdom come on earth, in the name of Jesus; may it come in our own bodies and broken hearts, as it is in heaven. Be poor in spirit and seek his kingdom first, and all those other things will be added to you.[19]

Siblings in the Wild Yard

I had been to Haiti and to Italy, but all I ever wanted was to be home. It's funny how traveling far away can be the thing that brings you close. While I was in Tuscany, I observed nature as if my Isaac lived inside my brain. If I saw an animal or a plant, I took notes in my journal, and then I sat at the computer as soon as I could to study what I had seen so I could tell him all about it. We saw a snake and lizards and many different birds. The fauna and the flora nearly undid me. I love nature, and I carried my nature-loving son in my heart.

I had gathered so much information about Italian wildlife that by the time I had him in my arms, I couldn't report it all. I just cried. I had simply missed him and his brothers so much. I imagined Ian building duomos with legos. I imagined Jude noticing the shadows in the art and Titus with the little boys in the stone streets.

When finally together again as the six of us, something settled in me, an idea conceived that felt like the blooming of new life. What I wanted was a simple thing, something I would have told you before Tuscany. I decided to love my life and to be satisfied in Jesus. I wanted to live as his friend. I wanted to believe the love of my Father, to be his girl child. I wanted to love my husband and be with my children while they are small. I wanted to live small, make choices that acknowledge the small in community, and I wanted to love what I do. I wanted kingdom to come in my real life, to see God more clearly through every metaphor. These desires were suddenly things to live instead of things to ponder.

I told myself that I would like to enjoy a very small house on an acre so we could learn the metaphors of the seed. So I opened the computer, and in the search box I filled in some blanks, a low dollar number, and narrowed the search by acreage. One single property fit the bill. It was a tiny ranch house with hardwood floors, an acre with a huge garden, a vintage kitchen, and rows of fruit and nut tress. I emailed the link to Seth, and within a day we visited the little green house, the only house we considered. We made an offer, and the offer was accepted. We moved there about six weeks later without a hitch.

This little piece of land felt like home before I made it five feet into the living room. It smelled like my mama Lois's house, like coffee and cake tins and ripe fruit. The attic fan reminded me of my grandmother. The pecan hulls' tannins told my nose right away that I was home, as much as I could understand it.

But when I realized that the huge backyard bled into the church parking lot of a tiny Church of Christ congregation— a congregation like the one of my youth—I cried, and I knew Jesus was very present in my thinking. He was all over me, like the jab of a brother and a loving kiss at once. I felt the nudge of a pair of commandments: "Love the Lord your God with all your heart and with all your soul and with all your mind," and "Love your neighbor as yourself."[1] How I act out everything I believe hinges on these two commandments.

Of course it does; now my neighbor is a congregation of the church body against whom I rebelled, the one with whom I wanted to cancel every association. So much of my faith journey has been a running away from what the members of these congregations have thought of me, because I had always assumed they had deemed me unacceptable. It took me years to raise my arms in worship how I longed to do without considering what they would think. I hadn't realized my harbored thoughts—"I am too much for them to handle." This was my excuse to withhold myself, and as I write this, I feel the old divide.

On moving day, the kind preacher helped us unload the truck. Then we began meeting the neighbors and, slowly, the members. One of the church elders lives on the other side of the church building, and he has invited the boys to shoot all the squirrels they want. Another older member is a neighbor too, and he's been whittling little razorbacks out of peach pits since he was four years old. With sun-spotted hands and a knife cutting delicate features, he leaned toward the boys with the tiny pig to show them. The boys wanted to be able to say that they, too, knew how to use a knife. The life in their eyes, of both the older men and our younger boys, revealed something of kin between them, something of the innocence allowed at home.

Before church starts, the kids show up and tap on our back sliding-glass door. My boys run out happy with them to the basketball court. On Wednesday nights, we join them for pizza, and from time to time we stay for Bible study. The discussion is as humble as I've heard in any living room. Our first topic was about unconditional love. I tensed at the thought of it and assumed to know what to expect: how many strings attach to *unconditional*. One said, "The churches of Christ often know the Scripture, but they are not always very good at loving unconditionally." I couldn't believe the weakness, the poverty of spirit. They were familiar like siblings who lie down on front steps to get quiet for what they might hear. The a cappella singing at the end of the night wasn't easy on the ears, but it still nearly made me cry, my kin. The same hymns that spoke to me of Jesus as a child are rising from the air next door to me three times a week.

We aren't members there, but they are our neighbor. I don't assume to know what they would think of me anymore, were I to lay my theology out on paper bare for all to see, but I don't assume to know what I would think of me either a year ago or two years from now. We're all changing, but God isn't. Kingdom isn't. I only know that when they invite us to dinner or when their little ones knock on the door asking to play with my boys, it's the kingdom of God at work. There's a kindness and a gentleness working itself out in our yard, and I know what it's like to be the mother looking on my children as they love one another.

When Isaac carried a pair of flower shears across the backyard to the tool shed, his grip loosened, and they fell point down straight into the top of his foot, so deep that he cut nerves. The preacher was the one who heard him cry, and he ran across the garden and carried him to the water hose. Isaac's foot poured blood, and the preacher washed it even from his face. He comforted him and delivered him through the back door to my mother. This is what the people of Jesus look like: washed and washing.

From the backyard, we wave to them. There's a clothesline between two massive trees that give us shade at every time of the day. Somehow the land is shaped there for a constant and gentle breeze. This is where we sit. We've been waiting for a gentle time. Coming out here to hang the clothes reminds me of my barefooted mama on a yellow trapeze, holding pins in her mouth, the sheets and her dress waving like summer flags. It reminds me of my sister putting a june bug in a snuff can, how we sang at the top of our lungs from the highest step on the blue pool slide. When there's time to hang on a line, to straighten the pants legs and listen to the kids laugh, then there's time to look up and see it; freedom flashes from our eyes.

I have made my laundry smell like lavender, and I hold the wet towels to my nose before hanging each one. I just turned on the sprinklers for a mound of strawberries with wilty heads, and the four boys are playing nearby. I see them have the thought, not about the clean clothes they wear but about how wide the water darts across the yard, and with four great, happy squeals, they run in together and hold their faces to the water and sling their hair around wet. They hold hands and run and laugh so hard that they hit the ground, covered up in loose grass and dirt. Their clothes peel off and land splat on the ground, a shirt in the compost pile.

They pay me no mind except to say, "Look, Mama! The sprinkler!" Every open pass through the water is a shout that we are home. We are children, and we are home. I squat nearby at a different angle, where the orange sun is directly behind them, and I watch their silhouettes shadow dance on a backdrop of glory.

Back at the line, I cry the tears of a woman satisfied that she has seen her children be free. In this one moment, I have seen my children run naked and wild. I have seen them without a drop of shame.

The culmination of all desire is not in marriage, motherhood, this yard, or the church building yonder. The Spirit of the Lord whispers it in quiet, empty places. We are loved. Yes, where the Sprit of the Lord is, the kingdom comes. Where the Spirit of the Lord is, there is freedom, and even in a little Arkansas yard, I see through to it, the wilderness redeemed, the hollow filled wild with Eden.

I pick up each towel and pin them slowly, like I'd never done anything more fulfilling, and I laugh at how he knows me, to move me to this yard at this time. How he must love me to have said no to so many other things to bring me here. At this clothesline, I am myself a child. Love bears down on me like a smile, like the sun, and it's warm and simple, just how I smile on the ones running through the garden. This is the kingdom, to see like a child, to live loved with my siblings, to work and to dance and to be filled up like a hollow, howl of laughter, fruit of joy.

Acknowledgments

So much life happened during the writing of this book, and the team at Revell has given me all the grace needed to live as freely as possible. I can't thank you enough for believing in me and with me. Also, how can an agent be such a sister and friend? Jenni Burke, I love you.

Mama and Daddy, you are my first metaphors for God, the garden, and the feast. Thank you for making my sister and my brothers. Thank you to Erin May, Will Carothers, and Scott Carothers. I don't know myself without you. You have taught me the most about the church, how different we are, how if you're not well, it makes me sick. If I am glad, you always feel it too. Ours is the best laugh. We are friends like E.T. and Eliot, only I'm pretty sure in that scenario I would be E.T. When I phone home, it's to you.

There was once a small group of friends who met on the floor of living rooms with us. We were all so poor then, weren't we? Thank you, old friends, for teaching the broken hallelujahs.

For the rare friendships of Ginny Mooney, Nicole Tatum, Lindsey Mason, Brooke Robinson, Hope Ray, Leslie Massey, Rebekah Lyons, Kelly Nikondeha, Tsh Oxenreider, Kevin Still, Becky Carter, and Elizabeth Milton—in feast or famine, even when I don't show up, thank you for always keeping room for me at your table, especially as I wrote this book.

Thank you to the Rays, Rusches, Markleys, Yanceys, and Livesays. You are the friends of recovery. You are the friends of communion.

If I ever felt that I needed to do something crazy, something like break open a jar of my most expensive perfume to pour on a beautiful set of feet, there is a group of subversive women who would help me pick up the glass and slam it to the ground. You know who you are: you roguely innocent, brave, and tender bunch of women. When I march, you are by my side. You smell like wild orange to me, all of you.

The two groups with whom I traveled in 2014 to Haiti and to Italy were folks whose quiet conversations showed me glory. You showed me your uncovered faces, how far pulled back is the veil. Thank you.

To my boys who can't read this yet because they are small: when it's time, you must know that you have shown me Jesus. Isaac, you teach me awe and wonder. When the fog settles midway down on the mountain, you see God. Tender is your strength. You mourn with those who mourn and laugh with those who laugh. Jude, the way you see the world is something that can't be taught. You have the gift of reading metaphors. You know the fertile ground of weakness and the burning desire of God. Ian, you assume best things. You are a lover of a cornerstone and a builder of walls that won't fall, because you build with joy. You are a speaker of blessing that sticks. You never run out of ways to worship. Titus, you are strong and courageous. You will tear down things that do need to fall. You are coming into wisdom and are strong of heart. Of all people on this planet, you four will have forgiven me most. You four are so good at love. Thank you for loving me.

Half the time I'm writing, I hardly know what I'm saying, but my husband has eyes for me. Seth sees the threads pulling through, sees the hand of God weaving. He sees the best version of me, us, my work, and our children. Thank you, Seth. We have no good recipes. We feign advice. Sometimes all we know to do is sing. *There's a wideness in God's mercy, like the wideness of the sea.* My favorite thing about my whole life is that I'm in the wide sea with you, love. Thank you for always bringing me the water.

Notes

Chapter 1 Rebel

1. This quote from Easy is shared with permission.

Chapter 2 Capacity: One

1. Matthew 11:29.
2. Philippians 2:6–8.

Chapter 3 Becoming Kin

1. Romans 11:36.

Chapter 4 A Harness on the Wind

1. 1 Corinthians 12:8 NET.
2. 1 Corinthians 8:1.
3. John 1:1.
4. John 1:14 ESV.
5. Luke 24:49 NLT.
6. Matthew 22:39.
7. Psalm 14:3 NIV.

Chapter 5 Hungry

1. James 1:14–15 ESV.
2. Isaiah 55:1.

Chapter 12 Seed of Desire

1. Galatians 5:22–23.
2. 1 John 4:18.
3. Deuteronomy 6:5.
4. 1 Corinthians 12:8–10; Ephesians 4:7–13; Romans 12:3–8.
5. James 1:21 ESV.
6. James 1:22.
7. 2 Corinthians 1:5.
8. John 16:33.

Chapter 13 See Through

1. 1 Corinthians 14:1.
2. 2 Corinthians 4:18.
3. Hosea 14:4 ESV.
4. Hebrews 11:3 ESV.
5. John 12:24; 1 Corinthians 15:36.
6. 1 Corinthians 4:20; Luke 24:49.
7. Hebrews 12:18–29.

Chapter 14 Hope of the Exiled

1. Matthew 23:10.
2. Matthew 5:3.
3. Luke 6:45.
4. 2 Corinthians 7:10.
5. Ephesians 6:12.
6. Luke 17:20–21 ESV.
7. Romans 14:17 ESV.
8. Matthew 4:1–11.
9. Isaiah 55:1–3 ESV.

Chapter 15 Whole in Sick Places

1. Matthew 6:33.
2. Matthew 6:10 KJV.